THE EIGHTEENTH BRUMAIRE
OF LOUIS BONAPARTE

KARL MARX

THE EIGHTEENTH BRUMAIRE OF LOUIS BONAPARTE

With Explanatory Notes

INTERNATIONAL PUBLISHERS

NEW YORK

PUBLISHER'S NOTE

This translation of *The Eighteenth Brumaire of Louis Bonaparte* by Karl Marx is based on the second edition (Hamburg, 1869), which was corrected by Karl Marx, and has been checked with the first edition (New York, 1852) and with the third edition (Hamburg, 1885). The present edition has also been checked with an earlier translation, edited by C. P. Dutt.

This Printing, 1972

ISBN: 0-7178-0056-3

Library of Congress Catalog Card Number: 63-23036

Printed in the United States of America

CONTENTS

Die Revolution,

Eine Zeitschrift in zwanglosen Heften.

Herausgegeben von

J. Weydemeyer.

Erstes Heft.

Der 18te Brumaire des Louis Napoleon

von

Karl Marx.

New-York.

Expedition: Deutsche Vereins-Buchhandlung von Schmidt und Helmich.
William-Street Nr. 191.

1852.

The title page of *Die Revolution*, the magazine that first published *The Eighteenth Brumaire of Louis Bonaparte*

THE EIGHTEENTH BRUMAIRE
OF LOUIS BONAPARTE[1]

AUTHOR'S PREFACE TO THE SECOND EDITION

My friend *Joseph Weydemeyer*,* whose death was so untimely, intended to publish a political weekly in New York starting from January 1, 1852. He invited me to provide this weekly with a history of the *coup d'état*. Down to the middle of February, I accordingly wrote him weekly articles under the title: *The Eighteenth Brumaire of Louis Bonaparte*. Meanwhile Weydemeyer's original plan had fallen through. Instead, in the spring of 1852 he began to publish a monthly, *Die Revolution*, the first number of which consists of my *Eighteenth Brumaire*. A few hundred copies of this found their way into Germany at that time, without, however, getting into the actual book trade. A German bookseller of extremely radical pretensions to whom I offered the sale of my book was most virtuously horrified at a "presumption" so "contrary to the times."

From the above facts it will be seen that the present work took shape under the immediate pressure of events and its historical material does not extend beyond the month of February (1852). Its re-publication now is due in part to the demand of the book trade, in part to the urgent requests of my friends in Germany.

Of the writings dealing with the same subject approximately *at the same time* as mine, only two deserve notice: Victor Hugo's *Napoléon le Petit* [*Napoleon the Little*] and Proudhon's *Coup d'Etat*.

---

* Military commandant of the St. Louis district during the American Civil War. [*Note by Marx.*]

Victor Hugo confines himself to bitter and witty invective against the responsible publisher of the *coup d'état*. The event itself appears in his work like a bolt from the blue. He sees in it only the violent act of a single individual. He does not notice that he makes this individual great instead of little by ascribing to him a personal power of initiative such as would be without parallel in world history. Proudhon, for his part, seeks to represent the *coup d'état* as the result of an antecedent historical development. Unnoticeably, however, his historical construction of the *coup d'état* becomes a historical *apologia* for its hero. Thus he falls into the error of our so-called *objective* historians. I, on the contrary, demonstrate how the *class struggle* in France created circumstances and relationships that made it possible for a grotesque mediocrity to play a hero's part.

A revision of the present work would have robbed it of its peculiar colouring. Accordingly I have confined myself to mere correction of printer's errors and to striking out allusions now no longer intelligible.

The concluding words of my work: "But when the imperial mantle finally falls on the shoulders of Louis Bonaparte, the bronze statue of Napoleon will crash from the top of the Vendôme Column," have already been fulfilled.

Colonel Charras opened the attack on the Napoleon cult in his work on the campaign of 1815. Subsequently, and particularly in the last few years, French literature made an end of the Napoleon legend with the weapons of historical research, of criticism, of satire and of wit. Outside France this violent breach with the traditional popular belief, this tremendous mental revolution, has been little noticed and still less understood.

Lastly, I hope that my work will contribute towards eliminating the school-taught phrase now current, particularly in Germany, of so-called *Caesarism*. In this superficial historical analogy the main point is forgotten, nameiy, that in ancient Rome the class struggle took place only within a privileged minority, between the free rich and the free poor, while the great productive mass of the population, the slaves, formed the purely passive pedestal for these combatants. People forget *Sismondi's* significant saying: The Roman proletariat lived at the expense of society, while modern society lives at the expense of the proletariat. With so complete a difference between the material, economic conditions of the ancient and the modern class struggles, the political figures produced by them can likewise have no more in common with one another than the Archbishop of Canterbury has with the High Priest Samuel.

KARL MARX

London, June 23, 1869

The fact that a new edition of *The Eighteenth Brumaire* has become necessary, thirty-three years after its first appearance, proves that even today this little book has lost none of its value.

It was in truth a work of genius. Immediately after the event that struck the whole political world like a thunderbolt from the blue, that was condemned by some with loud cries of moral indignation and accepted by others as salvation from the revolution and as punishment for its errors, but was only wondered at by all and understood by none—immediately after this event Marx came out with a concise, epigrammatic exposition that laid bare the whole course of French history since the February days in its inner interconnection, reduced the miracle of December 2 to a natural, necessary result of this interconnection and in so doing did not even need to treat the hero of the *coup d'état* otherwise than with the contempt he so well deserved. And the picture was drawn with such a master hand that every fresh disclosure since made has only provided fresh proofs of how faithfully it reflected reality. This eminent understanding of the living history of the day, this clear-sighted appreciation of events at the moment of happening, is indeed without parallel.

But for this, Marx's thorough knowledge of French history was needed. France is the land where, more than anywhere else, the historical class struggles were each time fought out to a decision, and where, consequently, the changing political forms within which they move and in which their results are summarized have been stamped in the sharpest outlines. The centre of feudalism in the Middle Ages, the model country of unified monarchy, resting on estates, since the Renaissance, France demolished feudalism in the Great Revolution and established the unalloyed rule of the bourgeoisie in a classical purity unequalled by any other European land. And the struggle of the upward-striving proletariat against the ruling bourgeoisie appeared here in an acute form unknown elsewhere. This was the reason why Marx not only studied the past history of France with particular predilection, but also followed her current history in every detail, stored up the material for future use and, consequently, events never took him by surprise.

In addition, however, there was still another circumstance. It was precisely Marx who had first discovered the great law of motion of history, the law according to which all historical struggles, whether they proceed in the political, religious, philosophical or some other ideological domain, are in fact only the more or less clear expression of struggles of social classes, and that the existence and thereby the collisions, too, between these classes are in turn conditioned by the degree of development of their economic position, by the mode of their production and of their exchange determined by it. This law, which has the same significance for history as the law of the transformation of energy has for natural science—this law gave him here, too, the key to an understanding of the history of the Second French Republic. He put his law to the test on these historical events, and even after thirty-three years we must still say that it has stood the test brilliantly.

FREDERICK ENGELS

I

Hegel remarks somewhere that all facts and personages of great importance in world history occur, as it were, twice. He forgot to add: the first time as tragedy, the second as farce. Caussidière for Danton, Louis Blanc for Robespierre, the *Montagne* of 1848 to 1851[2] for the *Montagne* of 1793 to 1795, the Nephew for the Uncle. And the same caricature occurs in the circumstances attending the second edition of the eighteenth Brumaire![3]

Men make their own history, but they do not make it just as they please; they do not make it under circumstances chosen by themselves, but under circumstances directly encountered, given and transmitted from the past. The tradition of all the dead generations weighs like a nightmare on the brain of the living. And just when they seem engaged in revolutionizing themselves and things, in creating something that has never yet existed, precisely in such periods of revolutionary crisis they anxiously conjure up the spirits of the past to their service and borrow from them names, battle cries and costumes in order to present the new scene of world history in this time-honoured disguise and this borrowed language. Thus Luther donned the mask of the Apostle Paul, the Revolution of 1789 to 1814 draped itself alternately as the Roman republic and the Roman empire, and the Revolution of 1848 knew nothing better to do than to parody, now 1789, now the revolutionary tradition of 1793 to 1795. In like manner a beginner who has learnt a new language always translates it back into his mother tongue, but he has assimilated the spirit of the new language and can freely express him-

15

self in it only when he finds his way in it without recalling the old and forgets his native tongue in the use of the new.

Consideration of this conjuring up of the dead of world history reveals at once a salient difference. Camille Desmoulins, Danton, Robespierre, Saint-Just, Napoleon, the heroes as well as the parties and the masses of the old French Revolution, performed the task of their time in Roman costume and with Roman phrases, the task of unchaining and setting up modern *bourgeois* society. The first ones knocked the feudal basis to pieces and mowed off the feudal heads which had grown on it. The other created inside France the conditions under which alone free competition could be developed, parcelled landed property exploited and the unchained industrial productive power of the nation employed; and beyond the French borders he everywhere swept the feudal institutions away, so far as was necessary to furnish bourgeois society in France with a suitable up-to-date environment on the European Continent. The new social formation once established, the antediluvian Colossi disappeared and with them resurrected Romanity—the Brutuses, Gracchi, Publicolas, the tribunes, the senators, and Caesar himself. Bourgeois society in its sober reality had begotten its true interpreters and mouthpieces in the Says, Cousins, Royer-Collards, Benjamin Constants and Guizots; its real military leaders sat behind the office desks, and the hog-headed Louis XVIII was its political chief. Wholly absorbed in the production of wealth and in peaceful competitive struggle, it no longer comprehended that ghosts from the days of Rome had watched over its cradle. But unheroic as bourgeois society is, it nevertheless took heroism, sacrifice, terror, civil war and battles of peoples to bring it into being. And in the classically austere traditions of the Roman republic its gladiators found the ideals and the art forms, the self-deceptions that they needed in order to conceal from themselves the bourgeois limitations of the content of their struggles and to keep their enthusiasm on the high plane of the great historical tragedy. Similarly, at another stage of development, a century earlier, Cromwell and the English people had borrowed speech, passions and illusions from the Old Testament for their bourgeois revolution. When the real aim had been achieved, when the bourgeois transformation of English society had been accomplished, Locke supplanted Habakkuk.

Thus the awakening of the dead in those revolutions served the purpose of glorifying the new struggles, not of parodying the old; of magnifying the given task in imagination, not of fleeing from its solution in reality; of finding once more the spirit of revolution, not of making its ghost walk about again.

From 1848 to 1851 only the ghost of the old revolution walked about, from Marrast, the *républicain en gants jaunes*,* who disguised himself as the old Bailly, down to the adventurer, who hides his commonplace repulsive features under the iron death mask of Napoleon. An entire people, which had imagined that by means of a revolution it had imparted to itself an accelerated power of motion, suddenly finds itself set back into a defunct epoch and, in order that no doubt as to the relapse may be possible, the old dates arise again, the old chronology, the old names, the old edicts, which had long become a subject of antiquarian erudition, and the old minions of the law, who had seemed long decayed. The nation feels like that mad Englishman in Bedlam who fancies that he lives in the times of the ancient Pharaohs and daily bemoans the hard labour that he must perform in the Ethiopian mines as a gold digger, immured in this subterranean prison, a dimly burning lamp fastened to his head, the overseer of the slaves behind him with a long whip, and at the exits a confused welter of barbarian mercenaries, who understand neither the forced labourers in the mines nor one another, since they speak no common language. "And all this is

---

* Republican in kid gloves.—*Ed.*

expected of me," sighs the mad Englishman, "of me, a free-born Briton, in order to make gold for the old Pharaohs." "In order to pay the debts of the Bonaparte family," sighs the French nation. The Englishman, so long as he was in his right mind, could not get rid of the fixed idea of making gold. The French, so long as they were engaged in revolution, could not get rid of the memory of Napoleon, as the election of December 10[4] proved. They hankered to return from the perils of revolution to the fleshpots of Egypt,[5] and December 2, 1851 was the answer. They have not only a caricature of the old Napoleon, they have the old Napoleon himself, caricatured as he must appear in the middle of the nineteenth century.

The social revolution of the nineteenth century cannot draw its poetry from the past, but only from the future. It cannot begin with itself before it has stripped off all superstition in regard to the past. Earlier revolutions required recollections of past world history in order to drug themselves concerning their own content. In order to arrive at its own content, the revolution of the nineteenth century must let the dead bury their dead. There the phrase went beyond the content; here the content goes beyond the phrase.

The February Revolution was a surprise attack, a *taking* of the old society *unawares*, and the people proclaimed this unexpected *stroke* as a deed of world importance, ushering in a new epoch. On December 2 the February Revolution is conjured away by a cardsharper's trick, and what seems overthrown is no longer the monarchy but the liberal concessions that were wrung from it by centuries of struggle. Instead of *society* having conquered a new content for itself, it seems that the *state* only returned to its oldest form, to the shamelessly simple domination of the sabre and the cowl. This is the answer to the *coup de main** of February 1848, given by the *coup de tête*** of De-

---

* *Coup de main*: Unexpected stroke.—*Ed.*
** *Coup de tête*: Rash act.—*Ed.*

cember 1851. Easy come, easy go. Meanwhile the interval of time has not passed by unused. During the years 1848 to 1851 French society has made up, and that by an abbreviated because revolutionary method, for the studies and experiences which, in a regular, so to speak, textbook course of development would have had to precede the February Revolution, if it was to be more than a ruffling of the surface. Society now seems to have fallen back behind its point of departure; it has in truth first to create for itself the revolutionary point of departure, the situation, the relations, the conditions under which alone modern revolution becomes serious.

Bourgeois revolutions, like those of the eighteenth century, storm swiftly from success to success; their dramatic effects outdo each other; men and things seem set in sparkling brilliants; ecstasy is the everyday spirit; but they are short-lived; soon they have attained their zenith, and a long crapulent depression lays hold of society before it learns soberly to assimilate the results of its storm-and-stress period. On the other hand, proletarian revolutions, like those of the nineteenth century, criticize themselves constantly, interrupt themselves continually in their own course, come back to the apparently accomplished in order to begin it afresh, deride with unmerciful thoroughness the inadequacies, weaknesses and paltrinesses of their first attempts, seem to throw down their adversary only in order that he may draw new strength from the earth and rise again, more gigantic, before them, recoil ever and anon from the indefinite prodigiousness of their own aims, until a situation has been created which makes all turning back impossible, and the conditions themselves cry out:

> Hic Rhodus, hic salta!
> Here is the rose, here dance![6]

For the rest, every fairly competent observer, even if he had not followed the course of French developments step by step, must have had a presentiment that an unheard-of fiasco was in store for the revolution. It was enough to hear the self-complacent howl of victory with which Messieurs the Democrats congratulated each other on the expected gracious consequences of the second Sunday in May 1852.[7] In their minds the second Sunday in May 1852 had become a fixed idea, a dogma, like the day on which Christ should reappear and the millennium begin, in the minds of the Chiliasts.[8] As ever, weakness had taken refuge in a belief in miracles, fancied the enemy overcome when he was only conjured away in imagination, and it lost all understanding of the present in a passive glorification of the future that was in store for it and of the deeds it had *in petto* but which it merely did not want to carry out as yet. Those heroes who seek to disprove their demonstrated incapacity by mutually offering each other their sympathy and getting together in a crowd had tied up their bundles, collected their laurel wreaths in advance and were just then engaged in discounting on the exchange market the republics *in partibus*[9] for which they had already providently organized the government personnel with all the calm of their unassuming disposition. December 2 struck them like a thunderbolt from a clear sky, and the peoples that in periods of pusillanimous depression gladly let their inward apprehension be drowned by the loudest bawlers will perchance have convinced themselves that the times are past when the cackle of geese could save the Capitol.

The Constitution, the National Assembly, the dynastic parties, the blue and the red republicans, the heroes of Africa, the thunder from the platform, the sheet lightning of the daily press, the entire literature, the political names and the intellectual reputations, the civil law and the penal code, the *liberté, égalité, fraternité* and the second Sunday in May 1852—all has vanished like a phantasmagoria before the spell of a man whom even his enemies do not make out to be a sorcerer. Universal suffrage seems to have survived only for a moment, in order that with its own hand it may make its last will and testament before the eyes of all the world and declare in the name of the people itself: All that exists deserves to perish.[10]

It is not enough to say, as the French do, that their nation was taken unawares. A nation and a woman are not forgiven the unguarded hour in which the first adventurer that came along could violate them. The riddle is not solved by such turns of speech, but merely formulated differently. It remains to be explained how a nation of thirty-six millions can be surprised and delivered unresisting into captivity by three *chevaliers d'industrie*.

Let us recapitulate in general outline the phases that the French Revolution went through from February 24, 1848, to December 1851.

Three main periods are unmistakable: *the February period*; May 4, 1848, to May 28, 1849[11]: *the period of the constitution of the republic*, or *of the Constituent National Assembly*; May 28, 1849, to December 2, 1851: *the period of the constitutional republic* or *of the Legislative National Assembly*.

The *first period*, from February 24, or the overthrow of Louis Philippe, to May 4, 1848, the meeting of the Constituent Assembly, the *February period* proper, may be described as the *prologue* to the revolution. Its character was officially expressed in the fact that the government improvised by it itself declared that it was *provisional* and, like the government, everything that was mooted, attempted or enunciated during this period proclaimed itself to be only *provisional*. Nothing and nobody ventured to lay claim to the right of existence and of real action. All the elements that had prepared or determined the revolution, the dynastic opposition,[12] the republican bourgeoisie, the democratic-republican petty bourgeoisie and the social-democratic workers, provisionally found their place in the February *government*.

It could not be otherwise. The February days originally

intended an electoral reform, by which the circle of the politically privileged among the possessing class itself was to be widened and the exclusive domination of the aristocracy of finance overthrown. When it came to the actual conflict, however, when the people mounted the barricades, the National Guard maintained a passive attitude, the army offered no serious resistance and the monarchy ran away, the republic appeared to be a matter of course. Every party construed it in its own way. Having secured it arms in hand, the proletariat impressed its stamp upon it and proclaimed it to be a *social republic*. There was thus indicated the general content of the modern revolution, a content which was in most singular contradiction to everything that, with the material available, with the degree of education attained by the masses, under the given circumstances and relations, could be immediately realized in practice. On the other hand, the claims of all the remaining elements that had collaborated in the February Revolution were recognized by the lion's share that they obtained in the government. In no period do we, therefore, find a more confused mixture of high-flown phrases and actual uncertainty and clumsiness, of more enthusiastic striving for innovation and more deeply-rooted domination of the old routine, of more apparent harmony of the whole of society and more profound estrangement of its elements. While the Paris proletariat still revelled in the vision of the wide prospects that had opened before it and indulged in seriously-meant discussions on social problems, the old powers of society had grouped themselves, assembled, reflected and found unexpected support in the mass of the nation, the peasants and petty bourgeois, who all at once stormed on to the political stage, after the barriers of the July Monarchy had fallen.

The *second period,* from May 4, 1848, to the end of May 1849, is the period of the *constitution,* the *foundation, of the bourgeois republic.* Directly after the February days not only had the dynastic opposition been surprised by the republicans and the republicans by the Socialists, but all France by Paris. The National Assembly, which met on May 4, 1848, had emerged from the national elections and represented the nation. It was a living protest against the pretensions of the February days and was to reduce the results of the revolution to the bourgeois scale. In vain the Paris proletariat, which immediately grasped the character of this National Assembly, attempted on May 15, a few days after it met, forcibly to negate its existence, to dissolve it, to disintegrate again into its constituent parts the organic form in which the proletariat was threatened by the reacting spirit of the nation. As is known, May 15 had no other result save that of removing Blanqui and his comrades, that is, the real leaders of the proletarian party, from the public stage for the entire duration of the cycle we are considering.

The *bourgeois monarchy* of Louis Philippe can be followed only by a *bourgeois republic*, that is to say, whereas a limited section of the bourgeoisie ruled in the name of the king, the whole of the bourgeoisie will now rule in the name of the people. The demands of the Paris proletariat are utopian nonsense, to which an end must be put. To this declaration of the Constituent National Assembly the Paris proletariat replied with the *June Insurrection,* the most colossal event in the history of European civil wars. The bourgeois republic triumphed. On its side stood the aristocracy of finance, the industrial bourgeoisie, the middle class, the petty bourgeois, the army, the *lumpenproletariat* organized as the Mobile Guard, the intellectual lights, the clergy and the rural population. On the side of the Paris proletariat stood none but itself. More than three thousand insurgents were butchered after the victory, and fifteen thousand were transported without trial. With this defeat the proletariat passes into the *background* of the revolutionary stage. It attempts to press forward again on every occasion, as soon as the movement appears to make a fresh start, but with ever decreased expenditure of strength and always slighter results. As soon as one of the social strata situated above it gets into revolutionary ferment, the proletariat enters into an alliance with it and so shares all the defeats that the different parties suffer, one after another. But these subsequent blows become the weaker, the greater the surface of society over which they are distributed. The more important leaders of the proletariat in the Assembly and in the press successively fall victims to the courts, and ever more equivocal figures come to head it. In part it throws itself into *doctrinaire experiments, exchange banks and workers' associations, hence into a movement in which it renounces the revolutionizing of the old world by means of the latter's own great, combined resources, and seeks, rather, to achieve its salvation behind society's back, in private fashion, within its limited conditions of existence, and hence necessarily suffers shipwreck.* It seems to be unable either to rediscover revolutionary greatness in itself or to win new energy from the connections newly entered into, until *all classes* with which it contended in June themselves lie prostrate beside it. But at least it succumbs with the honours of the great, world-historic struggle; not only France, but all Europe trembles at the June earthquake, while the ensuing defeats of the upper classes are so cheaply bought that they require bare-faced exaggeration by the victorious party to be able to pass for events at all, and become the more ignominious the further the defeated party is removed from the proletarian party.

The defeat of the June insurgents, to be sure, had now prepared, had levelled the ground on which the bourgeois republic could be founded and built up, but it had shown at the same time that in Europe the questions at issue are other than that of "republic or monarchy." It had revealed that here *bourgeois republic* signifies the unlimited despotism of one class over other classes. It had proved that in countries with an old civilization, with a developed forma-

24

tion of classes, with modern conditions of production and with an intellectual consciousness in which all traditional ideas have been dissolved by the work of centuries, *the republic* signifies *in general only the political form of revolution of bourgeois society* and not its *conservative form of life*, as, for example, in the United States of North America, where, though classes already exist, they have not yet become fixed, but continually change and interchange their elements in constant flux, where the modern means of production, instead of coinciding with a stagnant surplus population, rather compensate for the relative deficiency of heads and hands, and where, finally, the feverish, youthful movement of material production, which has to make a new world its own, has left neither time nor opportunity for abolishing the old spirit world.

During the June days all classes and parties had united in the *party of Order* against the proletarian class as the *party of Anarchy*, of Socialism, of Communism. They had "saved" society from "*the enemies of society*." They had given out the watchwords of the old society, "*property, family, religion, order,*" to their army as passwords and had proclaimed to the counter-revolutionary crusaders: "In this sign thou shalt conquer!" From that moment, as soon as one of the numerous parties which had gathered under this sign against the June insurgents seeks to hold the revolutionary battlefield in its own class interest, it goes down before the cry: "Property, family, religion, order." Society is saved just as often as the circle of its rulers contracts, as a more exclusive interest is maintained against a wider one. Every demand of the simplest bourgeois financial reform, of the most ordinary liberalism, of the most formal republicanism, of the most shallow democracy, is simultaneously castigated as an "attempt on society" and stigmatized as "Socialism." And, finally, the high priests of "the religion and order" themselves are driven with kicks from their Pythian tripods, hauled out of their beds in the darkness of night, put in prison-vans, thrown into dungeons or sent into exile; their temple is razed to the ground, their mouths are sealed, their pens broken, their law torn to pieces in the name of religion, of property, of the family, of order. Bourgeois fanatics for order are shot down on their balconies by mobs of drunken soldiers, their domestic sanctuaries profaned, their houses bombarded for amusement—in the name of property, of the family, of religion and of order. Finally, the scum of bourgeois society forms the *holy phalanx of order* and the hero Crapulinski[13] installs himself in the Tuileries as the *"saviour of society."*

II

Let us pick up the threads of the development once more. The history of the *Constituent National Assembly* since the June days is the *history of the domination and the disintegration of the republican faction of the bourgeoisie,* of that faction which is known by the names of tricolour republicans, pure republicans, political republicans, formalist republicans, etc.

Under the bourgeois monarchy of Louis Philippe it had formed the *official* republican *opposition* and consequently a recognized component part of the political world of the day. It had its representatives in the Chambers and a considerable sphere of influence in the press. Its Paris organ, the *National*,[14] was considered just as respectable in its way as the *Journal des Débats*.[15] Its character corresponded to this position under the constitutional monarchy. It was not a faction of the bourgeoisie held together by great common interests and marked off by specific conditions of production. It was a clique of republican-minded bourgeois, writers, lawyers, officers and officials that owed its influence to the personal antipathies of the country against Louis Philippe, to memories of the old republic, to the republican faith of a number of enthusiasts, above all, however, to *French nationalism,* whose hatred of the Vienna treaties and of the alliance with England it stirred up perpetually. A large part of the following that the *National* had under Louis Philippe was due to this concealed imperialism, which could consequently confront it later, under the republic, as a deadly rival in the person of Louis

Bonaparte. It fought the aristocracy of finance, as did all the rest of the bourgeois opposition. Polemics against the budget, which were closely connected in France with fighting the aristocracy of finance, procured popularity too cheaply and material for puritanical leading articles too plentifully, not to be exploited. The industrial bourgeoisie was grateful to it for its slavish defence of the French protectionist system, which it accepted, however, more on national grounds than on grounds of national economy; the bourgeoisie as a whole, for its vicious denunciation of Communism and Socialism. For the rest, the party of the *National* was *purely republican,* that is, it demanded a republican instead of a monarchist form of bourgeois rule and, above all, the lion's share of this rule. Concerning the conditions of this transformation it was by no means clear in its own mind. On the other hand, what was clear as daylight to it and was publicly acknowledged at the reform banquets in the last days of Louis Philippe, was its unpopularity with the democratic petty bourgeois and, in particular, with the revolutionary proletariat. These pure republicans, as is, indeed, the way with pure republicans, were already on the point of contenting themselves in the first instance with a regency of the Duchess of Orleans, when the February Revolution broke out and assigned their best-known representatives a place in the Provisional Government. From the start, they naturally had the confidence of the bourgeoisie and a majority in the Constituent National Assembly. The *socialist* elements of the Provisional Government were excluded forthwith from the Executive Commission which the National Assembly formed when it met, and the party of the *National* took advantage of the outbreak of the June insurrection to discharge the *Executive Commission* also, and therewith to get rid of its closest rivals, the *petty-bourgeois,* or *democratic, republicans* (Ledru-Rollin, etc.). Cavaignac, the general of the bourgeois-republican party who commanded the June massacre, took the place of the Executive Commission with a sort of dictatorial power. Marrast, former editor-in-chief of the *National*, became the perpetual president of the Constituent National Assembly, and the ministries, as well as all other important posts, fell to the portion of the pure republicans.

The republican bourgeois faction, which had long regarded itself as the legitimate heir of the July Monarchy, thus found its fondest hopes exceeded; it attained power, however, not as it had dreamed under Louis Philippe, through a liberal revolt of the bourgeoisie against the throne, but through a rising of the proletariat against capital, a rising laid low with grape-shot. What it had conceived as the *most revolutionary* event turned out in reality to be the *most counter-revolutionary*. The fruit fell into its lap, but it fell from the tree of knowledge, not from the tree of life.

The exclusive *rule of the bourgeois republicans* lasted only from June 24 to December 10, 1848. It is summed up in the *drafting of a republican constitution* and in the *state of siege of Paris*.

The new *Constitution* was at bottom only the republicanized edition of the constitutional Charter of 1830.[16] The narrow electoral qualification of the July Monarchy, which excluded even a large part of the bourgeoisie from political rule, was incompatible with the existence of the bourgeois republic. In lieu of this qualification, the February Revolution had at once proclaimed direct universal suffrage. The bourgeois republicans could not undo this event. They had to content themselves with adding the limiting proviso of a six months' residence in the constituency. The old organization of the administration, of the municipal system, of the judicial system, of the army, etc., continued to exist inviolate, or, where the Constitution changed them, the change concerned the table of contents, not the contents; the name, not the subject matter.

The inevitable general staff of the liberties of 1848, personal liberty, liberty of the press, of speech, of association, of assembly, of education and religion, etc., received a constitutional uniform, which made them invulnerable. For each of these liberties is proclaimed as the *absolute* right of the French *citoyen*, but always with the marginal note that it is unlimited so far as it is not limited by the "*equal rights of others* and the *public safety*" or by "laws" which are intended to mediate just this harmony of the individual liberties with one another and with the public safety. For example: "The citizens have the right of association, of peaceful and unarmed assembly, of petition and of expressing their opinions, whether in the press or in any other way. *The enjoyment of these rights has no limit save the equal rights of others and the public safety.*" (Chapter II of the French Constitution, §8.)—"Education is free. Freedom of education shall be *enjoyed* under the conditions fixed by law and under the supreme control of the state." (*Ibidem*, §9.)—"The home of every citizen is inviolable *except* in the forms prescribed by law." (Chapter II, §3.) Etc., etc.—The Constitution, therefore, constantly refers to future *organic* laws which are to put into effect those marginal notes and regulate the enjoyment of these unrestricted liberties in such manner that they will collide neither with one another nor with the public safety. And later, these organic laws were brought into being by the friends of order and all those liberties regulated in such manner that the bourgeoisie in its enjoyment of them finds itself unhindered by the equal rights of the other classes. Where it forbids these liberties entirely to "the others" or permits enjoyment of them under conditions that are just so many police traps, this always happens solely in the interest of "*public safety*," that is, the safety of the bourgeoisie, as the Constitution prescribes. In the sequel, both sides accordingly appeal with complete justice to the Constitution: the friends of order, who abrogated all these liberties, as well as the democrats, who demanded all of them. For each paragraph of the Constitution contains its own antithesis, its own Upper and Lower

House, namely, liberty in the general phrase, abrogation of liberty in the marginal note. Thus, so long as the *name* of freedom was respected and only its actual realization prevented, of course in a legal way, the constitutional existence of liberty remained intact, inviolate, however mortal the blows dealt to its existence *in actual life.*

This Constitution, made inviolable in so ingenious a manner, was nevertheless, like Achilles, vulnerable in one point, not in the heel, but in the head, or rather in the two heads in which it wound up—the *Legislative Assembly,* on the one hand, the *President,* on the other. Glance through the Constitution and you will find that only the paragraphs in which the relationship of the President to the Legislative Assembly is defined are absolute, positive, noncontradictory, and cannot be distorted. For here it was a question of the bourgeois republicans safeguarding themselves. §§45-70 of the Constitution are so worded that the National Assembly can remove the President constitutionally, whereas the President can remove the National Assembly only unconstitutionally, only by setting aside the Constitution itself. Here, therefore, it challenges its forcible destruction. It not only sanctifies the division of powers, like the Charter of 1830, it widens it into an intolerable contradiction. The *play of the constitutional powers,* as Guizot termed the parliamentary squabble between the legislative and executive power, is in the Constitution of 1848 continually played *va-banque.** On one side are seven hundred and fifty representatives of the people, elected by universal suffrage and eligible for re-election; they form an uncontrollable, indissoluble, indivisible National Assembly, a National Assembly that enjoys legislative omnipotence, decides in the last instance on war, peace and commercial treaties, alone possesses the right of amnesty and, by its permanence, perpetually holds the front of the stage. On the other side is the President, with

---

* *Va-banque:* Staking one's all.—*Ed.*

31

all the attributes of royal power, with authority to appoint and dismiss his ministers independently of the National Assembly, with all the resources of the executive power in his hands, bestowing all posts and disposing thereby in France of the livelihoods of at least a million and a half people, for so many depend on the five hundred thousand officials and officers of every rank. He has the whole of the armed forces behind him. He enjoys the privilege of pardoning individual criminals, of suspending National Guards, of discharging, with the concurrence of the Council of State, general, cantonal and municipal councils elected by the citizens themselves. Initiative and direction are reserved to him in all treaties with foreign countries. While the Assembly constantly performs on the boards and is exposed to daily public criticism, he leads a secluded life in the Elysian Fields, and that with Article 45 of the Constitution before his eyes and in his heart, crying to him daily: *"Frère, il faut mourir!"*[17] Your power ceases on the second Sunday of the lovely month of May in the fourth year after your election! Then your glory is at an end, the piece is not played twice and if you have debts, look to it betimes that you pay them off with the six hundred thousand francs granted you by the Constitution, unless, perchance, you should prefer to go to Clichy[18] on the second Monday of the lovely month of May!—Thus, whereas the Constitution assigns actual power to the President, it seeks to secure moral power for the National Assembly. Apart from the fact that it is impossible to create a moral power by paragraphs of law, the Constitution here abrogates itself once more by having the President elected by all Frenchmen through direct suffrage. While the votes of France are split up among the seven hundred and fifty members of the National Assembly, they are here, on the contrary, concentrated on a single individual. While each separate representative of the people represents only this or that party, this or that town, this or that bridgehead, or even only the mere necessity of electing some one as the seven hundred and fiftieth, without examining too closely either the cause or the man, *he* is the elect of the nation and the act of his election is the trump that the sovereign people plays once every four years. The elected National Assembly stands in a metaphysical relation, but the elected President in a personal relation, to the nation. The National Assembly, indeed, exhibits in its individual representatives the manifold aspects of the national spirit, but in the President this national spirit finds its incarnation. As against the Assembly, he possesses a sort of divine right; he is President by the grace of the people.

Thetis, the sea goddess, had prophesied to Achilles that he would die in the bloom of youth. The Constitution, which, like Achilles, had its weak spot, had also, like Achilles, its presentiment that it must go to an early death. It was sufficient for the constitution-making pure republicans to cast a glance from the lofty heaven of their ideal republic at the profane world to perceive how the arrogance of the royalists, the Bonapartists, the Democrats, the Communists as well as their own discredit grew daily in the same measure as they approached the completion of their great legislative work of art, without Thetis on this account having to leave the sea and communicate the secret to them. They sought to cheat destiny by a catch in the Constitution, through §111 of it, according to which every motion for a *revision of the Constitution* must be supported by at least three-quarters of the votes, cast in three successive debates between which an entire month must always lie, with the added proviso that not less than five hundred members of the National Assembly must vote. Thereby they merely made the impotent attempt still to exercise a power—when only a parliamentary minority, as which they already saw themselves prophetically in their mind's eye—a power which at the present time, when they commanded a parliamentary majority and all the resources of governmental authority, was slipping daily more and more from their feeble hands.

Finally the Constitution, in a melodramatic paragraph, entrusts itself "to the vigilance and the patriotism of the whole French people and every single Frenchman," after it had previously entrusted in another paragraph the "vigilant" and "patriotic" to the tender, most painstaking care of the High Court of Justice, the *"haute cour,"* invented by it for the purpose.

Such was the Constitution of 1848, which on December 2, 1851, was not overthrown by a head, but fell down at the touch of a mere hat; this hat, to be sure, was a three-cornered Napoleonic hat.

While the bourgeois republicans in the Assembly were busy devising, discussing and voting this Constitution, Cavaignac outside the Assembly maintained the *state of siege of Paris.* The state of siege of Paris was the midwife of the Constituent Assembly in its travail of republican creation. If the Constitution is subsequently put out of existence by bayonets, it must not be forgotten that it was likewise by bayonets, and these turned against the people, that it had to be protected in its mother's womb and by bayonets that it had to be brought into existence. The forefathers of the "respectable republicans" had sent their symbol, the tricolour, on a tour round Europe. They themselves in turn produced an invention that of itself made its way over the whole Continent, but returned to France with ever renewed love until it has now become naturalized in half her Departments—the *state of siege.* A splendid invention, periodically employed in every ensuing crisis in the course of the French Revolution. But barrack and bivouac, which were thus periodically laid on French society's head to compress its brain and render it quiet; sabre and musket, which were periodically allowed to act as judges and administrators, as guardians and censors, to play policeman and do night watchman's duty; moustache and uniform, which were periodically trumpeted forth as the highest wisdom of society and as its rector— were not barrack and bivouac, sabre and musket, moustache and uniform finally bound to hit upon the idea of rather saving society once and for all by proclaiming their own regime as the highest and freeing civil society completely from the trouble of governing itself? Barrack and bivouac, sabre and musket, moustache and uniform were bound to hit upon this idea all the more as they might then also expect better cash payment for their higher services, whereas from the merely periodical state of siege and the transient rescues of society at the bidding of this or that bourgeois faction little of substance was gleaned save some killed and wounded and some friendly bourgeois grimaces. Should not the military at last one day play state of siege in their own interest and for their own benefit, and at the same time besiege the citizens' purses? Moreover, be it noted in passing, one must not forget that *Colonel Bernard*, the same military commission president who under Cavaignac had 15,000 insurgents deported without trial, is at this moment again at the head of the military commissions active in Paris.

Whereas, with the state of siege in Paris, the respectable, the pure republicans planted the nursery in which the praetorians[19] of December 2, 1851 were to grow up, they on the other hand deserve praise for the reason that, instead of exaggerating the national sentiment as under Louis Philippe, they now, when they had command of the national power, crawled before foreign countries, and, instead of setting Italy free, let her be reconquered by Austrians and Neapolitans.[20] Louis Bonaparte's election as President on December 10, 1848, put an end to the dictatorship of Cavaignac and to the Constituent Assembly.

In §44 of the Constitution it is stated: "The President of the French Republic must never have lost his status of a French citizen." The first President of the French republic, L. N. Bonaparte, had not merely lost his status of a French citizen, had not only been an English special constable, he was even a naturalized Swiss.[21]

I have worked out elsewhere the significance of the election of December 10.[22] I will not revert to it here. It is sufficient to remark here that it was a *reaction of the peasants,* who had had to pay the costs of the February Revolution, against the remaining classes of the nation, a *reaction of the country against the town.* It met with great approval in the army, for which the republicans of the *National* had provided neither glory nor additional pay, among the big bourgeoisie, which hailed Bonaparte as a bridge to monarchy, among the proletarians and petty bourgeois, who hailed him as a scourge for Cavaignac. I shall have an opportunity later of going more closely into the relationship of the peasants to the French Revolution.

The period from December 20, 1848, until the dissolution of the Constituent Assembly, in May 1849, comprises the history of the downfall of the bourgeois republicans. After having founded a republic for the bourgeoisie, driven the revolutionary proletariat out of the field and reduced the democratic petty bourgeoisie to silence for the time being, they are themselves thrust aside by the mass of the bourgeoisie, which justly impounds this republic as *its property.* This bourgeois mass was, however, *royalist.* One section of it, the large landowners, had ruled during the *Restoration* and was accordingly *Legitimist.* The other, the aristocrats of finance and big industrialists, had ruled during the July Monarchy and was consequently *Orleanist.*[23] The high dignitaries of the army, the university, the church, the bar, the academy and of the press were to be found on either side, though in various proportions. Here, in the bourgeois republic, which bore neither the name *Bourbon* nor the name *Orleans,* but the name *Capital,* they had found the form of state in which they could rule *conjointly.* The June Insurrection had already united them in the "party of Order."[24] Now it was necessary, in the first place, to remove the coterie of bourgeois republicans who still occupied the seats of the National Assembly. Just as brutal as these pure republicans had

36

been in their misuse of physical force against the people, just as cowardly, mealy-mouthed, broken-spirited and incapable of fighting were they now in their retreat, when it was a question of maintaining their republicanism and their legislative rights against the executive power and the royalists. I need not relate here the ignominious history of their dissolution. They did not succumb; they passed out of existence. Their history has come to an end forever, and, both inside and outside the Assembly, they figure in the following period only as memories, memories that seem to regain life whenever the mere name of Republic is once more the issue and as often as the revolutionary conflict threatens to sink down to the lowest level. I may remark in passing that the journal which gave its name to this party, the *National*, was converted to Socialism in the following period.

Before we finish with this period we must still cast a retrospective glance at the two powers, one of which annihilated the other on December 2, 1851, whereas from December 20, 1848, until the exit of the Constituent Assembly, they had lived in conjugal relations. We mean Louis Bonaparte, on the one hand, and the party of the coalesced royalists, the party of Order, of the big bourgeoisie, on the other. On acceding to the presidency, Bonaparte at once formed a ministry of the party of Order, at the head of which he placed Odilon Barrot, the old leader, *nota bene*, of the most liberal faction of the parliamentary bourgeoisie. M. Barrot had at last secured the ministerial portfolio, the spectre of which had haunted him since 1830, and what is more, the premiership in the ministry; but not, as he had imagined under Louis Philippe, as the most advanced leader of the parliamentary opposition, but with the task of putting a parliament to death, and as the confederate of all his arch-enemies, Jesuits and Legitimists. He brought the bride home at last, but only after she had been prostituted. Bonaparte seemed to efface himself completely. This party acted for him.

The very first meeting of the council of ministers resolved on the expedition to Rome, which, it was agreed, should be undertaken behind the back of the National Assembly and the means for which were to be wrested from it by false pretences. Thus they began by swindling the National Assembly and secretly conspiring with the absolutist powers abroad against the revolutionary Roman republic. In the same manner and with the same manoeuvres Bonaparte prepared his *coup* of December 2 against the royalist Legislative Assembly and its constitutional republic. Let us not forget that the same party which formed Bonaparte's ministry on December 20, 1848, formed the majority of the Legislative National Assembly on December 2, 1851.

In August the Constituent Assembly had decided to dissolve only after it had worked out and promulgated a whole series of organic laws that were to supplement the Constitution. On January 6, 1849, the party of Order had a deputy named Rateau move that the Assembly should let the organic laws go and rather decide on its *own dissolution*. Not only the ministry, with Odilon Barrot at its head, but all the royalist members of the National Assembly told it in bullying accents then that its dissolution was necessary for the restoration of credit, for the consolidation of order, for putting an end to the indefinite provisional arrangements and for establishing a definitive state of affairs; that it hampered the productivity of the new government and sought to prolong its existence merely out of malice; that the country was tired of it. Bonaparte took note of all this invective against the legislative power, learnt it by heart and proved to the parliamentary royalists, on December 2, 1851, that he had learnt from them. He reiterated their own catchwords against them.

The Barrot ministry and the party of Order went further. They caused *petitions to the National Assembly* to be made throughout France, in which this body was politely requested to decamp. They thus led the unorganized popular masses into the fire of battle against the National Assembly, the constitutionally organized expression of the people. They taught Bonaparte to appeal against the parliamentary assemblies to the people. At length, on January 29, 1849, the day had come on which the Constituent Assembly was to decide concerning its own dissolution. The National Assembly found the building where its sessions were held occupied by the military; Changarnier, the general of the party of Order, in whose hands the supreme command of the National Guard and troops of the line had been united, held a great military review in Paris, as if a battle were impending, and the royalists in coalition threateningly declared to the Constituent Assembly that force would be employed if it should prove unwilling. It was willing, and only bargained for a very short extra term of life. What was January 29 but the *coup d'état* of December 2, 1851, only carried out by the royalists with Bonaparte against the republican National Assembly? The gentlemen did not observe, or did not wish to observe, that Bonaparte availed himself of January 29, 1849, to have a portion of the troops march past him in front of the Tuileries, and seized with avidity on just this first public summoning of the military power against the parliamentary power to foreshadow Caligula.[25] They, to be sure, saw only their Changarnier.

A motive that particularly actuated the party of Order in forcibly cutting short the duration of the Constituent Assembly's life was the *organic* laws supplementing the Constitution, such as the education law, the law on religious worship, etc. To the royalists in coalition it was most important that they themselves should make these laws and not let them be made by the republicans, who had grown mistrustful. Among these organic laws, however, was also a law on the responsibility of the President of the republic. In 1851 the Legislative Assembly was occupied with the drafting of just such a law, when Bonaparte anticipated this *coup* with the *coup* of December 2.

What would the royalists in coalition not have given in their parliamentary winter campaign of 1851 to have found the Responsibility Law ready to hand, and drawn up, at that, by a mistrustful, hostile, republican Assembly!

After the Constituent Assembly had itself shattered its last weapon on January 29, 1849, the Barrot ministry and the friends of order hounded it to death, left nothing undone that could humiliate it and wrested from the impotent, self-despairing Assembly laws that cost it the last remnant of respect in the eyes of the public. Bonaparte, occupied with his fixed Napoleonic idea, was brazen enough to exploit publicly this degradation of the parliamentary power. For when on May 8, 1849, the National Assembly passed a vote of censure of the ministry because of the occupation of Civitavecchia by Oudinot, and ordered it to bring back the Roman expedition to its alleged purpose,[26] Bonaparte published the same evening in the *Moniteur*[27] a letter to Oudinot, in which he congratulated him on his heroic exploits and, in contrast to the ink-slinging parliamentarians, already posed as the generous protector of the army. The royalists smiled at this. They regarded him simply as their dupe. Finally, when Marrast, the President of the Constituent Assembly, believed for a moment that the safety of the National Assembly was endangered and, relying on the Constitution, requisitioned a colonel and his regiment, the colonel declined, cited discipline in his support and referred Marrast to Changarnier, who scornfully refused him with the remark that he did not like *baïonnettes intelligentes*.* In November 1851, when the royalists in coalition wanted to begin the decisive struggle with Bonaparte, they sought to put through in their notorious *Quaestors' Bill,*[28] the principle of the direct requisition of troops by the President of the National Assembly. One of their generals, Le Flô, had signed the

---

* Intellectual bayonets.—*Ed.*

bill. In vain did Changarnier vote for it and Thiers pay homage to the far-sighted wisdom of the former Constituent Assembly. The *War Minister, Saint-Arnaud,* answered him as Changarnier had answered Marrast—and to the acclamation of the *Montagne!*

Thus the *party of Order,* when it was not yet the National Assembly, when it was still only the ministry, had itself stigmatized the *parliamentary regime.* And it makes an outcry when December 2, 1851 banished this regime from France!

We wish it a happy journey.

III

On May 28, 1849, the Legislative National Assembly met. On December 2, 1851, it was dispersed. This period covers the span of life of the *constitutional, or parliamentary, republic.*

In the first French Revolution the rule of the *Constitutionalists* is followed by the rule of the *Girondists* and the rule of the *Girondists* by the rule of the *Jacobins.* Each of these parties relies on the more progressive party for support. As soon as it has brought the revolution far enough to be unable to follow it further, still less to go ahead of it, it is thrust aside by the bolder ally that stands behind it and sent to the guillotine. The revolution thus moves along an ascending line.

It is the reverse with the Revolution of 1848. The proletarian party appears as an appendage of the petty-bourgeois-democratic party. It is betrayed and dropped by the latter on April 16, May 15, and in the June days. The democratic party, in its turn, leans on the shoulders of the bourgeois-republican party. The bourgeois republicans no sooner believe themselves well established than they shake off the troublesome comrade and support themselves on the shoulders of the party of Order. The party of Order hunches its shoulders, lets the bourgeois republicans tumble and throws itself on the shoulders of armed force. It fancies it is still sitting on its shoulders when, one fine morning, it perceives that the shoulders have transformed themselves into bayonets. Each party kicks from behind at that driving forward and in front leans over towards the party which presses backwards. No wonder that in this ridiculous posture it loses its balance and, having made the inevitable grimaces, collapses with curious capers. The revolution thus moves in a descending line. It finds itself in this state of retrogressive motion before the last February barricade has been cleared away and the first revolutionary authority constituted.

The period that we have before us comprises the most motley mixture of crying contradictions: constitutionalists who conspire openly against the Constitution; revolutionists who are confessedly constitutional; a National Assembly that wants to be omnipotent and always remains parliamentary; a *Montagne* that finds its vocation in patience and counters its present defeats by prophesying future victories; royalists who form the *patres conscripti** of the republic and are forced by the situation to keep the hostile royal houses, to which they adhere, abroad, and the republic, which they hate, in France; an executive power that finds its strength in its very weakness and its respectability in the contempt that it calls forth; a republic that is nothing but the combined infamy of two monarchies, the Restoration and the July Monarchy, with an imperial label —alliances whose first proviso is separation; struggles whose first law is indecision; wild, inane agitation in the name of tranquillity, most solemn preaching of tranquillity in the name of revolution; passions without truth, truths without passion; heroes without heroic deeds, history without events; development, whose sole driving force seems to be the calendar, wearying with constant repetition of the same tensions and relaxations; antagonisms that periodically seem to work themselves up to a climax only to lose their sharpness and fall away without being able to resolve themselves; pretentiously paraded exertions and philistine terror at the danger of the world coming to an

---

* *Patres conscripti*: Senators.—*Ed.*

end, and at the same time the pettiest intrigues and court comedies played by the world redeemers, who in their *laisser aller** remind us less of the Day of Judgment than of the times of the Fronde—the official collective genius of France brought to naught by the artful stupidity of a single individual; the collective will of the nation, as often as it speaks through universal suffrage, seeking its appropriate expression through the inveterate enemies of the interests of the masses, until, at length, it finds it in the self-will of a filibuster. If any section of history has been painted grey on grey, it is this. Men and events appear as inverted Schlemihls,[29] as shadows that have lost their bodies. The revolution itself paralyzes its own bearers and endows only its adversaries with passionate forcefulness. When the "red spectre," continually conjured up and exorcised by the counter-revolutionaries, finally appears, it appears not with the Phrygian cap of anarchy on its head, but in the uniform of order, in *red breeches*.

We have seen that the ministry which Bonaparte installed on December 20, 1848, on his Ascension Day, was a ministry of the party of Order, of the Legitimist and Orleanist coalition. This Barrot-Falloux ministry had outlived the republican Constituent Assembly, whose term of life it had more or less violently cut short, and found itself still at the helm. Changarnier, the general of the allied royalists, continued to unite in his person the general command of the First Army Division and of the National Guard of Paris. Finally, the general elections had secured the party of Order a large majority in the National Assembly. Here the deputies and peers of Louis Philippe encountered a hallowed host of Legitimists, for whom many of the nation's ballots had become transformed into admission cards to the political stage. The Bonapartist representatives of the people were too sparse to be able to form an independent parliamentary party. They appeared

---

* *Laisser aller*: Letting things take their course.—*Ed.*

merely as the *mauvaise queue** of the party of Order. Thus the party of Order was in possession of the governmental power, the army and the legislative body, in short, of the whole of the state power; it had been morally strengthened by the general elections, which made its rule appear as the will of the people, and by the simultaneous triumph of the counter-revolution on the whole continent of Europe.

Never did a party open its campaign with greater resources or under more favourable auspices.

The shipwrecked *pure republicans* found that they had melted down to a clique of about fifty men in the Legislative National Assembly, the African generals Cavaignac, Lamoricière and Bedeau at their head. The great opposition party, however, was formed by the *Montagne.* The *social-democratic* party had given itself this parliamentary baptismal name. It commanded more than two hundred of the seven hundred and fifty votes of the National Assembly and was consequently at least as powerful as any one of the three factions of the party of Order taken by itself. Its numerical inferiority compared with the entire royalist coalition seemed compensated by special circumstances. Not only did the elections in the Departments show that it had gained a considerable following among the rural population. It counted in its ranks almost all the deputies from Paris; the army had made a confession of democratic faith by the election of three non-commissioned officers, and the leader of the *Montagne*, Ledru-Rollin, in contradistinction to all the representatives of the party of Order, had been raised to the parliamentary peerage by five Departments, which had pooled their votes for him. In view of the inevitable clashes of the royalists among themselves and of the whole party of Order with Bonaparte, the *Montagne* thus seemed to have all the elements of success before it on May 28, 1849. A fortnight later it had lost everything, honour included.

---

* *Mauvaise queue*: Evil appendage.—*Ed.*

Before we pursue parliamentary history further, some remarks are necessary to avoid common misconceptions regarding the whole character of the epoch that lies before us. Looked at with the eyes of democrats, the period of the Legislative National Assembly is concerned with what the period of the Constituent Assembly was concerned with: the simple struggle between republicans and royalists. The movement itself, however, they sum up in the one shibboleth: "*reaction*"—night, in which all cats are grey and which permits them to reel off their night watchman's commonplaces. And, to be sure, at first sight the party of Order reveals a maze of different royalist factions, which not only intrigue against each other—each seeking to elevate its own pretender to the throne and exclude the pretender of the opposing faction—but also all unite in common hatred of, and common onslaughts on, the "republic." In opposition to this royalist conspiracy the *Montagne*, for its part, appears as the representative of the "republic." The party of Order appears to be perpetually engaged in a "reaction," directed against press, association and the like, neither more nor less than in Prussia, and which, as in Prussia, is carried out in the form of brutal police intervention by the bureaucracy, the *gendarmerie* and the law courts. The *"Montagne,"* for its part, is just as continually occupied in warding off these attacks and thus defending the "eternal rights of man" as every so-called people's party has done, more or less, for a century and a half. If one looks at the situation and the parties more closely, however, this superficial appearance, which veils the *class struggle* and the peculiar physiognomy of this period, disappears.

Legitimists and Orleanists, as we have said, formed the two great factions of the party of Order. Was that which held these factions fast to their pretenders and kept them apart from one another nothing but lily and tricolour, House of Bourbon and House of Orleans, different shades of royalism, was it at all the confession of faith of royal-

46

ism? Under the Bourbons, *big landed property* had governed, with its priests and lackeys; under the Orleans, high finance, large-scale industry, large-scale trade, that is, *capital*, with its retinue of lawyers, professors and smooth-tongued orators. The Legitimate Monarchy was merely the political expression of the hereditary rule of the lords of the soil, as the July Monarchy was only the political expression of the usurped rule of the bourgeois *parvenus*. What kept the two factions apart, therefore, was not any so-called principles, it was their material conditions of existence, two different kinds of property, it was the old contrast between town and country, the rivalry between capital and landed property. That at the same time old memories, personal enmities, fears and hopes, prejudices and illusions, sympathies and antipathies, convictions, articles of faith and principles bound them to one or the other royal house, who denies this? Upon the different forms of property, upon the social conditions of existence, rises an entire superstructure of distinct and peculiarly formed sentiments, illusions, modes of thought and views of life. The entire class creates and forms them out of its material foundations and out of the corresponding social relations. The single individual, who derives them through tradition and upbringing, may imagine that they form the real motives and the starting point of his activity. While Orleanists and Legitimists, while each faction sought to make itself and the other believe that it was loyalty to their two royal houses which separated them, facts later proved that it was rather their divided interests which forbade the uniting of the two royal houses. And as in private life one differentiates between what a man thinks and says of himself and what he really is and does, so in historical struggles one must distinguish still more the phrases and fancies of parties from their real organism and their real interests, their conception of themselves, from their reality. Orleanists and Legitimists found themselves side by side in the republic, with equal claims.

47

If each side wished to effect the *restoration* of its *own* royal house against the other, that merely signified that each of the *two great interests* into which the *bourgeoisie* is split—landed property and capital—sought to restore its own supremacy and the subordination of the other. We speak of two interests of the bourgeoisie, for large landed property, despite its feudal coquetry and pride of race, has been rendered thoroughly bourgeois by the development of modern society. Thus the Tories in England long imagined that they were enthusiastic about monarchy, the church and the beauties of the old English Constitution, until the day of danger wrung from them the confession that they are enthusiastic only about *ground rent*.

The royalists in coalition carried on their intrigues against one another in the press, in Ems, in Claremont,[30] outside parliament. Behind the scenes they donned their old Orleanist and Legitimist liveries again and once more engaged in their old tourneys. But on the public stage, in their grand performances of state, as a great parliamentary party, they put off their respective royal houses with mere obeisances and adjourn the restoration of the monarchy *in infinitum*.* They do their real business as the *party of Order*, that is, under a *social*, not under a *political* title; as representatives of the bourgeois world-order, not as knights of errant princesses; as the bourgeois class against other classes, not as royalists against the republicans. And as the party of Order they exercised more unrestricted and sterner domination over the other classes of society than ever previously under the Restoration or under the July Monarchy, a domination which, in general, was only possible under the form of the parliamentary republic, for only under this form could the two great divisions of the French bourgeoisie unite, and thus put the rule of their class instead of the regime of a privileged faction of it on the order of the day. If, nevertheless, they, as the party of

* To infinity.—*Ed.*

48

Order, also insulted the republic and expressed their repugnance to it, this happened not merely from royalist memories. Instinct taught them that the republic, true enough, makes their political rule complete, but at the same time undermines its social foundation, since they must now confront the subjugated classes and contend against them without mediation, without the concealment afforded by the crown, without being able to divert the national interest by their subordinate struggles among themselves and with the monarchy. It was a feeling of weakness that caused them to recoil from the pure conditions of their own class rule and to yearn for the former more incomplete, more undeveloped and precisely on that account less dangerous forms of this rule. On the other hand, every time the royalists in coalition come in conflict with the pretender that confronts them, with Bonaparte, every time they believe their parliamentary omnipotence endangered by the executive power, every time, therefore, that they must produce their political title to their rule, they come forward as *republicans* and not as *royalists*, from the Orleanist Thiers, who warns the National Assembly that the republic divides them least, to the Legitimist Berryer, who, on December 2, 1851, as a tribune swathed in a tricoloured sash, harangues the people assembled before the town hall of the tenth *arrondissement* in the name of the republic. To be sure, a mocking echo calls back to him: Henry V! Henry V!

As against the coalesced bourgeoisie, a coalition between petty bourgeois and workers had been formed, the so-called *social-democratic* party. The petty bourgeois saw that they were badly rewarded after the June days of 1848, that their material interests were imperilled and that the democratic guarantees which were to ensure the effectuation of these interests were called in question by the counter-revolution. Accordingly, they came closer to the workers. On the other hand, their parliamentary representation, the *Montagne*, thrust aside during the dictatorship

49

of the bourgeois republicans, had in the last half of the life of the Constituent Assembly reconquered its lost popularity through the struggle with Bonaparte and the royalist ministers. It had concluded an alliance with the socialist leaders. In February 1849, banquets celebrated the reconciliation. A joint program was drafted, joint election committees were set up and joint candidates put forward. From the social demands of the proletariat the revolutionary point was broken off and a democratic turn given to them; from the democratic claims of the petty bourgeoisie the purely political form was stripped off and their socialist point thrust forward. Thus arose the *Social-Democracy*. The new *Montagne*, the result of this combination, contained, apart from some supernumeraries from the working class and some socialist sectarians, the same elements as the old *Montagne*, only numerically stronger. However, in the course of development, it had changed with the class that it represented. The peculiar character of the Social-Democracy is epitomized in the fact that democratic-republican institutions are demanded as a means, not of doing away with two extremes, capital and wage labour, but of weakening their antagonism and transforming it into harmony. However different the means proposed for the attainment of this end may be, however much it may be trimmed with more or less revolutionary notions, the content remains the same. This content is the transformation of society in a democratic way, but a transformation within the bounds of the petty bourgeoisie. Only one must not form the narrow-minded notion that the petty bourgeoisie, on principle, wishes to enforce an egoistic class interest. Rather, it believes that the *special* conditions of its emancipation are the *general* conditions within the frame of which alone modern society can be saved and the class struggle avoided. Just as little must one imagine that the democratic representatives are indeed all shopkeepers or enthusiastic champions of shopkeepers. According to their education and their individual position they may be as far apart as heaven from earth. What makes them representatives of the petty bourgeoisie is the fact that in their minds they do not get beyond the limits which the latter do not get beyond in life, that they are consequently driven, theoretically, to the same problems and solutions to which material interest and social position drive the latter practically. This is, in general, the relationship between the *political* and *literary representatives* of a class and the class they represent.

After the analysis given, it is obvious that if the *Montagne* continually contends with the party of Order for the republic and the so-called rights of man, neither the republic nor the rights of man are its final end, any more than an army which one wants to deprive of its weapons and which resists has taken the field in order to remain in possession of its own weapons.

Immediately, as soon as the National Assembly met, the party of Order provoked the *Montagne*. The bourgeoisie now felt the necessity of making an end of the democratic petty bourgeois, just as a year before it had realized the necessity of settling with the revolutionary proletariat. Only the situation of the adversary was different. The strength of the proletarian party lay in the streets, that of the petty bourgeois in the National Assembly itself. It was therefore a question of decoying them out of the National Assembly into the streets and causing them to smash their parliamentary power themselves, before time and circumstances could consolidate it. The *Montagne* rushed headlong into the trap.

The bombardment of Rome by the French troops was the bait that was thrown to it. It violated Article V of the Constitution[31] which forbids the French republic to employ its military forces against the freedom of another people. In addition to this, Article 54 prohibited any declaration of war on the part of the executive power without the assent of the National Assembly, and by its resolution of May 8, the Constituent Assembly had disapproved of the

Roman expedition. On these grounds Ledru-Rollin brought in a bill of impeachment against Bonaparte and his ministers on June 11, 1849. Exasperated by the wasp stings of Thiers, he actually let himself be carried away to the point of threatening that he would defend the Constitution by every means, even with arms in hand. The *Montagne* rose to a man and repeated this call to arms. On June 12, the National Assembly rejected the bill of impeachment, and the *Montagne* left the parliament. The events of June 13 are known: the proclamation issued by a section of the *Montagne*, declaring Bonaparte and his ministers "outside the Constitution"; the street procession of the democratic National Guards, who, unarmed as they were, dispersed on encountering the troops of Changarnier, etc., etc. A part of the *Montagne* fled abroad; another part was arraigned before the High Court at Bourges, and a parliamentary regulation subjected the remainder to the schoolmasterly surveillance of the President of the National Assembly. Paris was again declared in a state of siege and the democratic part of its National Guard dissolved. Thus the influence of the *Montagne* in parliament and the power of the petty bourgeois in Paris were broken.

Lyons, where June 13 had given the signal for a bloody insurrection of the workers, was, along with the five surrounding Departments, likewise declared in a state of siege, a condition that has continued up to the present moment.

The bulk of the *Montagne* had left its vanguard in the lurch, having refused to subscribe to its proclamation. The press had deserted, only two journals having dared to publish the *pronunciamento*. The petty bourgeois betrayed their representatives, in that the National Guards either stayed away or, where they appeared, hindered the erection of barricades. The representatives had duped the petty bourgeois, in that the alleged allies from the army were nowhere to be seen. Finally, instead of gaining an accession of strength from it, the democratic party had infected the proletariat with its own weakness and, as is usual with the great deeds of democrats, the leaders had the satisfaction of being able to charge their "people" with desertion, and the people the satisfaction of being able to charge its leaders with humbugging it.

Seldom had an action been announced with more noise than the impending campaign of the *Montagne*, seldom had an event been trumpeted with greater certainty or longer in advance than the inevitable victory of the democracy. Most assuredly, the democrats believe in the trumpets before whose blasts the walls of Jericho fell down. And as often as they stand before the ramparts of despotism, they seek to imitate the miracle. If the *Montagne* wished to triumph in parliament, it should not have called to arms. If it called to arms in parliament, it should not have acted in parliamentary fashion in the streets. If the peaceful demonstration was meant seriously, then it was folly not to foresee that it would be given a war-like reception. If a real struggle was intended, then it was a queer idea to lay down the weapons with which it would have to be waged. But the revolutionary threats of the petty bourgeois and their democratic representatives are mere attempts to intimidate the antagonist. And when they have run into a blind alley, when they have sufficiently compromised themselves to make it necessary to give effect to their threats, then this is done in an ambiguous fashion that avoids nothing so much as the means to the end and tries to find excuses for succumbing. The blaring overture that announced the contest dies away in a pusillanimous snarl as soon as the struggle has to begin, the actors cease to take themselves *au sérieux*, and the action collapses completely, like a pricked bubble.

No party exaggerates its means more than the democratic, none deludes itself more light-mindedly over the situation. Since a section of the army had voted for it, the *Montagne* was now convinced that the army would revolt for it. And on what occasion? On an occasion which, from the standpoint of the troops, had no other meaning than that the revolutionists took the side of the Roman soldiers against the French soldiers. On the other hand, the recollections of June 1848 were still too fresh to allow of anything but a profound aversion on the part of the proletariat towards the National Guard and a thorough-going mistrust of the democratic chiefs on the part of the chiefs of the secret societies. To iron out these differences, it was necessary for great, common interests to be at stake. The violation of an abstract paragraph of the Constitution could not provide these interests. Had not the Constitution been repeatedly violated, according to the assurance of the democrats themselves? Had not the most popular journals branded it as counter-revolutionary botch-work? But the democrat, because he represents the petty bourgeoisie, that is, a *transition class*, in which the interests of two classes are simultaneously mutually blunted, imagines himself elevated above class antagonism generally. The democrats concede that a privileged class confronts them, but they, along with all the rest of the nation, form the *people*. What they represent is the *people's rights*; what interests them is the *people's interests*. Accordingly, when a struggle is impending, they do not need to examine the interests and positions of the different classes. They do not need to weigh their own resources too critically. They have merely to give the signal and the *people*, with all its inexhaustible resources, will fall upon the *oppressors*. Now, if in the performance their interests prove to be uninteresting and their potency impotence, then either the fault lies with pernicious sophists, who split the *indivisible people* into different hostile camps, or the army was too brutalized and blinded to comprehend that the pure aims of democracy are the best thing for it itself, or the whole thing has been wrecked by a detail in its execution, or else an unforeseen accident has this time spoilt the game. In any case, the democrat comes out of the most disgraceful defeat just as immaculate as he was innocent when he went into it, with the newly-won conviction that he is bound to win, not that he himself and his party have to give up the old standpoint, but, on the contrary, that conditions have to ripen to suit him.

Accordingly, one must not imagine the *Montagne*, decimated and broken though it was, and humiliated by the new parliamentary regulation, as being particularly miserable. If June 13 had removed its chiefs, it made room, on the other hand, for men of lesser calibre, whom this new position flattered. If their impotence in parliament could no longer be doubted, they were entitled now to confine their actions to outbursts of moral indignation and blustering declamation. If the party of Order affected to see embodied in them, as the last official representatives of the revolution, all the terrors of anarchy, they could in reality be all the more insipid and modest. They consoled themselves, however, for June 13 with the profound utterance: But if they dare to attack universal suffrage, well then—then we'll show them what we are made of! *Nous verrons!**

So far as the *Montagnards* who fled abroad are concerned, it is sufficient to remark here that Ledru-Rollin, because in barely a fortnight he had succeeded in ruining irretrievably the powerful party at whose head he stood, now found himself called upon to form a French government *in partibus;*** that to the extent that the level of the revolution sank and the official bigwigs of official France became more dwarf-like, his figure in the distance, removed from the scene of action, seemed to grow in stature; that he could figure as the republican pretender for 1852, and that he issued periodical circulars to the Wallachians and other peoples, in which the despots of the Continent are threatened with the deeds of himself and his confederates. Was Proudhon altogether wrong when he cried to these gentlemen: *"Vous n'êtes que des blagueurs"?***

* We shall see!—*Ed.*
** Purely nominal.—*Ed.*
*** "You are nothing but windbags."—*Ed.*

On June 13, the party of Order had not only broken the *Montagne*, it had effected the *subordination of the Constitution to the majority decisions of the National Assembly.* And it understood the republic thus: that the bourgeoisie rules here in parliamentary forms, without, as in a monarchy, encountering any barrier such as the veto power of the executive or the right to dissolve parliament. This was a *parliamentary republic*, as Thiers termed it. But whereas on June 13 the bourgeoisie secured its omnipotence within the house of parliament, did it not afflict parliament itself, as against the executive authority and the people, with incurable weakness by expelling its most popular part? By surrendering numerous deputies without further ado on the demand of the courts, it abolished its own parliamentary immunity. The humiliating regulations to which it subjected the *Montagne* exalted the President of the republic in the same measure as it degraded the individual representatives of the people. By branding an insurrection for the protection of the constitutional charter an anarchic act aiming at the subversion of society, it precluded the possibility of its appealing to insurrection should the executive authority violate the Constitution in relation to it. And by the irony of history, the general who on Bonaparte's instructions bombarded Rome and thus provided the immediate occasion for the constitutional revolt of June 13, that *Oudinot* had to be the man offered by the party of Order imploringly and unavailingly to the people as general on behalf of the Constitution against Bonaparte on December 2, 1851. Another hero of June 13, *Vieyra,* who was lauded from the tribune of the National Assembly for the brutalities that he had committed in the democratic newspaper offices at the head of a gang of National Guards belonging to high finance circles—this same Vieyra had been initiated into Bonaparte's conspiracy and he essentially contributed to depriving the National Assembly in the hour of its death of any protection by the National Guard.

June 13 had still another meaning. The *Montagne* had wanted to force the impeachment of Bonaparte. Its defeat was therefore a direct victory for Bonaparte, his personal triumph over his democratic enemies. The party of Order gained the victory; Bonaparte had only to cash in on it. He did so. On June 14 a proclamation could be read on the walls of Paris in which the President, reluctantly, against his will, as it were, compelled by the sheer force of events, comes forth from his cloistered seclusion and, posing as misunderstood virtue, complains of the calumnies of his opponents and, while ₙe seems to identify his person with the cause of order, rather identifies the cause of order with his person. Moreover, the National Assembly had, it is true, subsequently approved the expedition against Rome, but Bonaparte had taken the initiative in the matter. After having re-installed the High Priest Samuel in the Vatican, he could hope to enter the Tuileries as King David.[32] He had won the priests over to his side.

The revolt of June 13 was confined, as we have seen, to a peaceful street procession. No war laurels were, therefore, to be won against it. Nevertheless, at a time as poor as this in heroes and events, the party of Order transformed this bloodless battle into a second Austerlitz. Platform and press praised the army as the power of order, in contrast to the popular masses, representing the impotence of anarchy, and extolled Changarnier as the "bulwark of society," a deception in which he himself finally came to believe. Surreptitiously, however, the corps that seemed doubtful were transferred from Paris, the regiments which had shown at the elections the most democratical sentiments were banished from France to Algiers, the turbulent spirits among the troops were relegated to penal detachments, and finally the isolation of the press from the barracks and of the barracks from bourgeois society was systematically carried out.

Here we have reached the decisive turning point in the history of the French National Guard. In 1830 it was decisive in the overthrow of the Restoration. Under Louis Philippe every rebellion miscarried in which the National Guard stood on the side of the troops. When in the February days of 1848 it evinced a passive attitude towards the insurrection and an equivocal one towards Louis Philippe, he gave himself up for lost and actually was lost. Thus the conviction took root that the revolution could not be victorious *without* the National Guard, nor the army *against* it. This was the superstition of the army in regard to civilian omnipotence. The June days of 1848, when the entire National Guard, with the troops of the line, put down the insurrection, had strengthened the superstition. After Bonaparte's assumption of office, the position of the National Guard was to some extent weakened by the unconstitutional union, in the person of Changarnier, of the command of its forces with the command of the First Army Division.

Just as the command of the National Guard appeared here as an attribute of the military commander-in-chief, so the National Guard itself appeared as only an appendage of the troops of the line. Finally, on June 13 its power was broken, and not only by its partial disbandment, which from this time on was periodically repeated all over France, until mere fragments of it were left behind. The demonstration of June 13 was, above all, a demonstration of the democratic National Guards. They had not, to be sure, borne their arms, but worn their uniforms against the army; precisely in this uniform, however, lay the talisman. The army convinced itself that this uniform was a piece of woollen cloth like any other. The spell was broken. In the June days of 1848, bourgeoisie and petty bourgeoisie had united as the National Guard with the army against the proletariat; on June 13, 1849, the bourgeoisie let the petty-bourgeois National Guard be dispersed by the army; on December 2, 1851, the National Guard of the bourgeoisie itself had vanished, and Bonaparte merely registered this fact when he subsequently signed the decree for its disbandment. Thus the bourgeoisie had itself smashed its last weapon against the army, the moment the petty bourgeoisie no longer stood behind it as a vassal, but before it as a rebel, it had to smash it as in general it was bound to destroy all its means of defence against absolutism with its own hand as soon as it had itself become absolute.

Meanwhile, the party of Order celebrated the reconquest of a power that seemed lost in 1848 only to be found again, freed from its restraints, in 1849, celebrated by means of invectives against the republic and the Constitution, of curses on all future, present and past revolutions, including that which its own leaders had made, and in laws by which the press was muzzled, association destroyed and the state of siege regulated as an organic institution. The National Assembly then adjourned from the middle of August to the middle of October, after having appointed a permanent commission for the period of its absence. During this recess the Legitimists intrigued with Ems, the Orleanists—with Claremont, Bonaparte—by means of princely tours, and the Departmental Councils—in deliberations on a revision of the Constitution: incidents which regularly recur in the periodic recesses of the National Assembly and which I propose to discuss only when they become events. Here it may merely be remarked, in addition, that it was impolitic for the National Assembly to disappear for considerable intervals from the stage and leave only a single, albeit a sorry, figure to be seen at the head of the republic, that of Louis Bonaparte, while to the scandal of the public the party of Order fell asunder into its royalist component parts and followed its conflicting desires for Restoration. As often as the confused noise of *parliament* grew silent during these recesses and its body dissolved in the nation, it became unmistakably clear that only one thing was still wanting to complete the true form of this republic: to make the *former's* recess permanent and replace the *latter's* inscription: Liberté, Égalité, Fraternité by the unambiguous words: Infantry, Cavalry, Artillery!

IV

In the middle of October 1849, the National Assembly met once more. On November 1, Bonaparte surprised it with a message in which he announced the dismissal of the Barrot-Falloux ministry and the formation of a new ministry. No one has ever sacked lackeys with less ceremony than Bonaparte his ministers. The kicks that were intended for the National Assembly were given in the meantime to Barrot and Co.

The Barrot ministry, as we have seen, had been composed of Legitimists and Orleanists, a ministry of the party of Order. Bonaparte had needed it to dissolve the republican Constituent Assembly, to bring about the expedition against Rome and to break the democratic party. Behind this ministry he had seemingly effaced himself, surrendered governmental power into the hands of the party of Order and donned the modest character mask that the responsible editor of a newspaper wore under Louis Philippe, the mask of the *homme de paille*.* He now threw off a mask which was no longer the light veil behind which he could hide his physiognomy, but an iron mask which prevented him from displaying a physiognomy of his own. He had appointed the Barrot ministry in order to blast the republican National Assembly in the name of the party of Order; he dismissed it in order to declare his own name independent of the National Assembly of the party of Order.

---

* *Homme de paille*: Man of straw.—*Ed.*

Plausible pretexts for this dismissal were not lacking. The Barrot ministry neglected even the decencies that would have let the President of the republic appear as a power side by side with the National Assembly. During the recess of the National Assembly Bonaparte published a letter to Edgar Ney in which he seemed to disapprove of the illiberal attitude of the Pope,* just as in opposition to the Constituent Assembly he had published a letter in which he commended Oudinot for the attack on the Roman republic. When the National Assembly now voted the budget for the Roman expedition, Victor Hugo, out of alleged liberalism, brought up this letter for discussion. The party of Order with scornfully incredulous outcries stifled the idea that Bonaparte's ideas could have any political importance. Not one of the ministers took up the gauntlet for him. On another occasion Barrot, with his well-known hollow rhetoric, let fall from the platform words of indignation concerning the "abominable intrigues" that, according to his assertion, went on in the immediate entourage of the President. Finally, while the ministry obtained from the National Assembly a widow's pension for the Duchess of Orleans it rejected any proposal to increase the Civil List of the President. And in Bonaparte the imperial pretender was so intimately bound up with the adventurer down on his luck that the one great idea, that he was called to restore the empire, was always supplemented by the other, that it was the mission of the French people to pay his debts.

The Barrot-Falloux ministry was the first and last *parliamentary ministry* that Bonaparte brought into being. Its dismissal forms, accordingly, a decisive turning-point. With it the party of Order lost, never to reconquer it, an indispensable post for the maintenance of the parliamentary regime, the lever of executive power. It is immediately obvious that in a country like France, where the execu-

---

tive power commands an army of officials numbering more than half a million individuals and therefore constantly maintains an immense mass of interests and livelihoods in the most absolute dependence; where the state enmeshes, controls, regulates, superintends and tutors civil society from its most comprehensive manifestations of life down to its most insignificant stirrings, from its most general modes of being to the private existence of individuals; where through the most extraordinary centralization this parasitic body acquires a ubiquity, an omniscience, a capacity for accelerated mobility and an elasticity which finds a counterpart only in the helpless dependence, in the loose shapelessness of the actual body politic —it is obvious that in such a country the National Assembly forfeits all real influence when it loses command of the ministerial posts, if it does not at the same time simplify the administration of the state, reduce the army of officials as far as possible and, finally, let civil society and public opinion create organs of their own, independent of the governmental power. But it is precisely with the maintenance of that extensive state machine in its numerous ramifications that the *material interests* of the French bourgeoisie are interwoven in the closest fashion. Here it finds posts for its surplus population and makes up in the form of state salaries for what it cannot pocket in the form of profit, interest, rents and honorariums. On the other hand, its *political interests* compelled it to increase daily the repressive measures and therefore the resources and the personnel of the state power, while at the same time it had to wage an uninterrupted war against public opinion and mistrustfully mutilate, cripple, the independent organs of the social movement, where it did not succeed in amputating them entirely. Thus the French bourgeoisie was compelled by its class position to annihilate, on the one hand, the vital conditions of all parliamentary power, and therefore, likewise, of its own, and to render irresistible, on the other hand, the executive power hostile to it.

The new ministry was called the d'Hautpoul ministry. Not in the sense that General d'Hautpoul had received the rank of Prime Minister. Rather, simultaneously with Barrot's dismissal, Bonaparte abolished this dignity, which, true enough, condemned the President of the republic to the status of the legal nonentity of a constitutional monarch, but of a constitutional monarch without throne or crown, without scepter or sword, without irresponsibility, without imprescriptible possession of the highest state dignity, and, worst of all, without a Civil List. The d'Hautpoul ministry contained only one man of parliamentary standing, the moneylender *Fould*, one of the most notorious of the high financiers. To his lot fell the ministry of finance. Look up the quotations on the Paris *bourse* and you will find that from November 1, 1849, onwards the French *fonds** rise and fall with the rise and fall of Bonapartist stocks. While Bonaparte had thus found his ally in the *bourse,* he at the same time took possession of the police by appointing Carlier Police Prefect of Paris.

Only in the course of development, however, could the consequences of the change of ministers come to light. To begin with, Bonaparte had taken a step forward only to be driven backward all the more conspicuously. His brusque message was followed by the most servile declaration of allegiance to the National Assembly. As often as the ministers dared to make a diffident attempt to introduce his personal fads as legislative proposals, they themselves seemed to carry out, against their will only and compelled by their position, comical commissions of whose fruitlessness they were persuaded in advance. As often as Bonaparte blurted out his intentions behind the ministers' backs and played with his *"idées napoléoniennes,"*[33] his own ministers disavowed him from the tribune of the National Assembly. His usurpatory longings seemed to make themselves heard only in order that the malicious laugh-

---

* *Fonds*: Government securities.—*Ed.*

ter of his opponents might not be muted. He behaved like an unrecognized genius, whom all the world takes for a simpleton. Never did he enjoy the contempt of all classes in fuller measure than during this period. Never did the bourgeoisie rule more absolutely, never did it display more ostentatiously the insignia of domination.

I have not here to write the history of its legislative activity, which is summarized during this period in two laws: in the law re-establishing the *wine tax* and the *education law* abolishing unbelief. If wine drinking was made harder for the French, they were presented all the more plentifully with the water of true life. If in the law on the wine tax the bourgeoisie declared the old, hateful French tax system to be inviolable, it sought through the education law to ensure among the masses the old state of mind that put up with the tax system. One is astonished to see the Orleanists, the liberal bourgeois, these old apostles of Voltairianism and eclectic philosophy, entrust to their hereditary enemies, the Jesuits, the superintendence of the French mind. However, in regard to the pretenders to the throne, Orleanists and Legitimists could part company, they understood that to secure their united rule necessitated the uniting of the means of repression of two epochs, that the means of subjugation of the July Monarchy had to be supplemented and strengthened by the means of subjugation of the Restoration.

The peasants, disappointed in all their hopes, crushed more than ever by the low level of grain prices on the one hand, and by the growing burden of taxes and mortgage debts on the other, began to bestir themselves in the Departments. They were answered by a drive against the schoolmasters, who were made subject to the clergy, by a drive against the *maires*,* who were made subject to the prefects, and by a system of espionage, to which all were made subject. In Paris and the large towns reaction itself

---

* *Maires*: Mayors.—*Ed.*

has the physiognomy of its epoch and challenges more than it strikes down. In the countryside it becomes dull, coarse, petty, tiresome and vexatious, in a word, the *gendarme*. One comprehends how three years of the regime of the *gendarme*, consecrated by the regime of the priest, were bound to demoralize immature masses.

Whatever amount of passion and declamation might be employed by the party of Order against the minority from the tribune of the National Assembly, its speech remained as monosyllabic as that of the Christians, whose words were to be: Yea, yea; nay, nay! As monosyllabic on the platform as in the press. Flat as a riddle whose answer is known in advance. Whether it was a question of the right of petition or the tax on wine, freedom of the press or free trade, the clubs or the municipal charter, protection of personal liberty or regulation of the state budget, the watchword constantly recurs, the theme remains always the same, the verdict is ever ready and invariably reads: "*Socialism!*" Even bourgeois liberalism is declared *socialistic,* bourgeois enlightenment socialistic, bourgeois financial reform socialistic. It was socialistic to build a railway, where a canal already existed, and it was socialistic to defend oneself with a cane when one was attacked with a rapier.

This was not merely a figure of speech, fashion or party tactics. The bourgeoisie had a true insight into the fact that all the weapons which it had forged against feudalism turned their points against itself, that all the means of education which it had produced rebelled against its own civilization, that all the gods which it had created had fallen away from it. It understood that all the so-called bourgeois liberties and organs of progress attacked and menaced its *class rule* at its social foundation and its political summit simultaneously, and had therefore become "*socialistic.*" In this menace and this attack it rightly discerned the secret of Socialism, whose import and tendency it judges more correctly than so-called Socialism knows how to judge itself; the latter can, accordingly, not comprehend why the bourgeoisie callously hardens its heart against it, whether it sentimentally bewails the sufferings of mankind, or in Christian spirit prophesies the millennium and universal brotherly love, or in humanistic style twaddles about mind, education and freedom, or in doctrinaire fashion excogitates a system for the conciliation and welfare of all classes. What the bourgeoisie did not grasp, however, was the logical conclusion that its *own parliamentary regime*, that its *political rule* in general, was now also bound to meet with the general verdict of condemnation as being *socialistic*. As long as the rule of the bourgeois class had not been organized completely, as long as it had not acquired its pure political expression, the antagonism of the other classes, likewise, could not appear in its pure form, and where it did appear could not take the dangerous turn that transforms every struggle against the state power into a struggle against capital. If in every stirring of life in society it saw "tranquillity" imperilled, how could it want to maintain at the head of society a *regime of unrest*, its own regime, the *parliamentary regime*, this regime that, according to the expression of one of its spokesmen, lives in struggle and by struggle? The parliamentary regime lives by discussion; how shall it forbid discussion? Every interest, every social institution, is here transformed into general ideas, debated as ideas; how shall any interest, any institution, sustain itself above thought and impose itself as an article of faith? The struggle of the orators on the platform evokes the struggle of the scribblers of the press; the debating club in parliament is necessarily supplemented by debating clubs in the salons and the pothouses; the representatives, who constantly appeal to public opinion, give public opinion the right to speak its real mind in petitions. The parliamentary regime leaves everything to the decision of majorities; how shall the great majorities outside parliament not want to decide? When you play the fiddle at the top of the state, what else is to be expected but that those down below dance?

Thus, by now stigmatizing as *"socialistic"* what it had previously extolled as *"liberal,"* the bourgeoisie confesses that its own interests dictate that it should be delivered from the danger of its *own rule*; that, in order to restore tranquillity in the country, its bourgeois parliament must, first of all, be given its quietus; that in order to preserve its social power intact, its political power must be broken; that the individual bourgeois can continue to exploit the other classes and to enjoy undisturbed property, family, religion and order only on condition that their class be condemned along with the other classes to like political nullity; that in order to save its purse, it must forfeit the crown, and the sword that is to safeguard it must at the same time be hung over its own head as a sword of Damocles.

In the domain of the interests of the general citizenry, the National Assembly showed itself so unproductive that, for example, the discussions on the Paris-Avignon railway, which began in the winter of 1850, were still not ripe for conclusion on December 2, 1851. Where it did not repress or pursue a reactionary course it was stricken with incurable barrenness.

While Bonaparte's ministry partly took the initiative in framing laws in the spirit of the party of Order, and partly even outdid that party's harshness in their execution and administration, he, on the other hand, by childishly silly proposals sought to win popularity, to bring out his opposition to the National Assembly, and to hint at a secret reserve that was only temporarily prevented by conditions from making its hidden treasures available to the French people. Such was the proposal to decree an increase in pay of four sous a day to the non-commissioned officers. Such was the proposal of an honour system loan bank for the workers. Money as a gift and money as a loan, it was with prospects such as these that he hoped to allure the masses. Donations and loans—the financial science of the *lumpenproletariat,* whether of high degree or low, is restricted to this. Such were the only springs which Bonaparte knew how to set in action. Never has a pretender speculated more stupidly on the stupidity of the masses.

The National Assembly flared up repeatedly over these unmistakable attempts to gain popularity at its expense, over the growing danger that this adventurer, whom his debts spurred on and no established reputation held back, would venture a desperate *coup*. The discord between the party of Order and the President had taken on a threatening character when an unexpected event threw him back repentant into its arms. We mean the *by-elections of March 10, 1850*. These elections were held for the purpose of filling the representatives' seats that after June 13 had been rendered vacant by imprisonment or exile. Paris elected only social-democratic candidates. It even concentrated most of the votes on an insurgent of June 1848, on Deflotte. Thus did the Parisian petty bourgeoisie, in alliance with the proletariat, revenge itself for its defeat on June 13, 1849. It seemed to have disappeared from the battlefield at the moment of danger only to reappear there on a more propitious occasion with more numerous fighting forces and with a bolder battle cry. One circumstance seemed to heighten the peril of this election victory. The army voted in Paris for the June insurgent against La Hitte, a minister of Bonaparte's, and in the Departments largely for the *Montagnards*, who here, too, though indeed not so decisively as in Paris, maintained the ascendancy over their adversaries.

Bonaparte saw himself suddenly confronted with revolution once more. As on January 29, 1849, as on June 13, 1849, so on March 10, 1850, he disappeared behind the party of Order. He made obeisance, he pusillanimously begged pardon, he offered to appoint any ministry it pleased at the behest of the parliamentary majority, he even implored the Orleanist and Legitimist party leaders, the Thiers, the Berryers, the Broglies, the Molés, in brief,

the so-called burgraves,[34] to take the helm of state themselves. The party of Order proved unable to take advantage of this opportunity that would never return. Instead
of boldly possessing itself of the power offered, it did not
even compel Bonaparte to reinstate the ministry dismissed on November 1; it contented itself with humiliating him by its forgiveness and adjoining M. *Baroche* to
the d'Hautpoul ministry. As public prosecutor this Baroche
had stormed and raged before the High Court at Bourges, the first time against the revolutionists of May 15, the
second time against the democrats of June 13, both times
because of an attempt on the life of the National Assembly. None of Bonaparte's ministers subsequently contributed more to the degradation of the National Assembly,
and after December 2, 1851, we meet him once more as the
comfortably installed and highly paid Vice-President of
the Senate. He had spat in the revolutionists' soup in order that Bonaparte might eat it up.

The social-democratic party, for its part, seemed only
to try to find pretexts for putting its own victory once
again in doubt and for blunting its point. Vidal, one of the
newly elected representatives of Paris, had been elected
simultaneously in Strasbourg. He was induced to decline
the election for Paris and accept it for Strasbourg. And
so, instead of making its victory at the polls conclusive
and thereby compelling the party of Order at once to contest it in parliament, instead of thus forcing the adversary to fight at the moment of popular enthusiasm and favourable mood in the army, the democratic party wearied
Paris during the months of March and April with a new
election campaign, let the aroused popular passions wear
themselves out in this repeated provisional election game,
let the revolutionary energy satiate itself with constitutional successes, dissipate itself in petty intrigues, hollow
declamations and sham movements, let the bourgeoisie
rally and make its preparations, and, lastly, weakened the
significance of the March elections by a sentimental com-

mentary in the April by-election, the election of Eugène Sue. In a word, it made an April Fool of March 10.

The parliamentary majority understood the weakness of its antagonist. Its seventeen burgraves—for Bonaparte had left to it the direction of and responsibility for the attack—drew up a new electoral law, the introduction of which was entrusted to M. Faucher, who solicited this honour for himself. On May 8 he introduced the law by which universal suffrage was to be abolished, a residence of three years in the locality of the election to be imposed as a condition on the electors and, finally, the proof of this residence made dependent in the case of workers on a certificate from their employers.

Just as the democrats had, in revolutionary fashion, agitated the minds and raged during the constitutional election contest, so now, when it was requisite to prove the serious nature of that victory arms in hand, did they in constitutional fashion preach order, majestic calm (*calme majestueux*), lawful action, that is to say, blind subjection to the will of the counter-revolution, which imposed itself as the law. During the debate the Mountain put the party of Order to shame by asserting, against the latter's revolutionary passionateness, the dispassionate attitude of the philistine who keeps within the law, and by felling that party to earth with the fearful reproach that it proceeded in a revolutionary manner. Even the newly elected deputies were at pains to prove by their decorous and discreet action what a misconception it was to decry them as anarchists and construe their election as a victory for revolution. On May 31, the new electoral law went through. The *Montagne* contented itself with smuggling a protest into the pocket of the President. The electoral law was followed by a new press law, by which the revolutionary newspaper press was entirely suppressed.[35] It had deserved its fate. The *National* and *La Presse*,[36] two bourgeois organs, were left behind after this deluge as the most advanced outposts of the revolution.

We have seen how during March and April the democratic leaders had done everything to embroil the people of Paris in a sham fight, how after May 8 they did everything to restrain them from a real fight. In addition to this, we must not forget that the year 1850 was one of the most splendid years of industrial and commercial prosperity, and the Paris proletariat was therefore fully employed. But the election law of May 31, 1850, excluded it from any participation in political power. It cut it off from the very arena of the struggle. It threw the workers back into the position of pariahs which they had occupied before the February Revolution. By letting themselves be led by the democrats in face of such an event and forgetting the revolutionary interests of their class for momentary ease and comfort, they renounced the honour of being a conquering power, surrendered to their fate, proved that the defeat of June 1848 had put them out of the fight for years and that the historical process would for the present again have to go on *over* their heads. So far as the petty-bourgeois democracy is concerned, which on June 13 had cried: "But if once universal suffrage is attacked, then we'll show them!", it now consoled itself with the contention that the counter-revolutionary blow which had struck it was no blow and the law of May 31 no law. On the second Sunday in May 1852, every Frenchman would appear at the polling place with ballot in one hand and sword in the other. With this prophecy it rested content. Lastly, the army was disciplined by its superior officers for the elections of March and April 1850, just as it had been disciplined for those of May 28, 1849. This time, however, it said decidedly: "The revolution shall not dupe us a third time."

The law of May 31, 1850, was the *coup d'état* of the bourgeoisie. All its conquests over the revolution hitherto had only a provisional character. They were endangered as soon as the existing National Assembly retired from the stage. They depended on the hazards of a new general election, and the history of elections since 1848 irrefutably proved that the bourgeoisie's moral sway over the mass of the people was lost in the same measure as its actual domination developed. On March 10, universal suffrage declared itself directly against the domination of the bourgeoisie; the bourgeoisie answered by outlawing universal suffrage. The law of May 31 was, therefore, one of the necessities of the class struggle. On the other hand, the Constitution required a minimum of two million votes to make an election of the President of the republic valid. If none of the candidates for the presidency received this minimum, the National Assembly was to choose the President from among the three candidates to whom the largest number of votes would fall. At the time when the Constituent Assembly made this law, ten million electors were registered on the rolls of voters. In its view, therefore, a fifth of the people entitled to vote was sufficient to make the presidential election valid. The law of May 31 struck at least three million votes off the electoral rolls, reduced the number of people entitled to vote to seven million and, nevertheless, retained the legal minimum of two million for the presidential election. It therefore raised the legal minimum from a fifth to nearly a third of the effective votes, that is, it did everything to smuggle the election of the President out of the hands of the people and into the hands of the National Assembly. Thus through the electoral law of May 31 the party of Order seemed to have made its rule doubly secure, by surrendering the election of the National Assembly and that of the President of the republic to the stationary section of society.

V

As soon as the revolutionary crisis had been weathered and universal suffrage abolished, the struggle between the National Assembly and Bonaparte broke out again.

The Constitution had fixed Bonaparte's salary at 600,000 francs. Barely six months after his installation he succeeded in increasing this sum to twice as much, for Odilon Barrot wrung from the Constituent National Assembly an extra allowance of 600,000 francs a year for so-called representation moneys. After June 13, Bonaparte had caused similar requests to be voiced, this time without eliciting response from Barrot. Now, after May 31, he at once availed himself of the favourable moment and caused his ministers to propose a Civil List of three millions in the National Assembly. A long life of adventurous vagabondage had endowed him with the most developed antennae for feeling out the weak moments when he might squeeze money from his bourgeois. He practised regular *chantage*.* The National Assembly had violated the sovereignty of the people with his assistance and his cognizance. He threatened to denounce its crime to the tribunal of the people unless it loosened its purse strings and purchased his silence with three million a year. It had robbed three million Frenchmen of their franchise. He demanded, for every Frenchman out of circulation, a franc in circulation, precisely three million francs. He, the elect of six millions, claimed damages for the votes out of which he said he had retrospectively been cheated. The Commission of the Na-

---

* *Chantage*: Blackmail.—*Ed.*

tional Assembly refused the importunate one. The Bonapartist press threatened. Could the National Assembly break with the President of the republic at a moment when in principle it had definitely broken with the mass of the nation? It rejected the annual Civil List, it is true, but it granted, for this once, an extra allowance of two million one hundred and sixty thousand francs. It thus rendered itself guilty of the double weakness of granting the money and of showing at the same time by its vexation that it granted it unwillingly. We shall see later for what purpose Bonaparte needed the money. After this vexatious aftermath, which followed on the heels of the abolition of universal suffrage and in which Bonaparte exchanged his humble attitude during the crisis of March and April for challenging impudence to the usurpatory parliament, the National Assembly adjourned for three months, from August 11 to November 11. In its place it left behind a Permanent Commission of twenty-eight members, which contained no Bonapartists, but did contain some moderate republicans. The Permanent Commission of 1849 had included only Order men and Bonapartists. But at that time the party of Order declared itself in permanence against the revolution. This time the parliamentary republic declared itself in permanence against the President. After the law of May 31, this was the only rival that still confronted the party of Order.

When the National Assembly met once more in November 1850, it seemed that, instead of the petty skirmishes it had hitherto had with the President, a great and ruthless struggle, a life-and-death struggle between the two powers, had become inevitable.

As in 1849 so during this year's parliamentary recess, the party of Order had broken up into its separate factions, each occupied with its own Restoration intrigues, which had obtained fresh nutriment through the death of Louis Philippe. The Legitimist king, Henry V, had even nominated a formal ministry which resided in Paris and in which members of the Permanent Commission held seats. Bonaparte, in his turn, was therefore entitled to make tours of the French Departments, and according to the disposition of the town that he favoured with his presence, now more or less covertly, now more or less overtly, to divulge his own restoration plans and canvass votes for himself. On these processions, which the great official *Moniteur* and the little private *Moniteurs* of Bonaparte naturally had to celebrate as triumphal processions, he was constantly accompanied by persons affiliated with the *Society of December 10*. This society dates from the year 1849. On the pretext of founding a benevolent society, the *lumpenproletariat* of Paris had been organized into secret sections, each section being led by Bonapartist agents, with a Bonapartist general at the head of the whole. Alongside decayed *roués* with dubious means of subsistence and of dubious origin, alongside ruined and adventurous offshoots of the bourgeoisie, were vagabonds, discharged soldiers, discharged jailbirds, escaped galley slaves, swindlers, mountebanks, *lazzaroni*, pickpockets, tricksters, gamblers, *maquereaus*,* brothel keepers, porters, *literati,* organ-grinders, ragpickers, knife grinders, tinkers, beggars—in short, the whole indefinite, disintegrated mass, thrown hither and thither, which the French term *la bohème*; from this kindred element Bonaparte formed the core of the Society of December 10. A "benevolent society"—in so far as, like Bonaparte, all its members felt the need of benefiting themselves at the expense of the labouring nation. This Bonaparte, who constitutes himself *chief of the lumpenproletariat*, who here alone rediscovers in mass form the interests which he personally pursues, who recognizes in this scum, offal, refuse of all classes the only class upon which he can base himself unconditionally, is the real Bonaparte, the Bonaparte *sans phrase*. An old crafty *roué*, he conceives the historical life of the na-

---

* *Maquereaus*: Procurers.—*Ed.*

tions and their performances of state as comedy in the most vulgar sense, as a masquerade where the grand costumes, words and postures merely serve to mask the pettiest knavery. Thus on his expedition to Strasbourg, where a trained Swiss vulture had played the part of the Napoleonic eagle. For his irruption into Boulogne he puts some London lackeys into French uniforms. They represent the army.[37] In his Society of December 10, he assembles ten thousand rascally fellows, who are to play the part of the people, as Nick Bottom that of the lion. At a moment when the bourgeoisie itself played the most complete comedy, but in the most serious manner in the world, without infringing any of the pedantic conditions of French dramatic etiquette, and was itself half deceived, half convinced of the solemnity of its own performance of state, the adventurer, who took the comedy as plain comedy, was bound to win. Only when he has eliminated his solemn opponent, when he himself now takes his imperial role seriously and under the Napoleonic mask imagines he is the real Napoleon, does he become the victim of his own conception of the world, the serious buffoon who no longer takes world history for a comedy but his comedy for world history. What the national *ateliers* were for the socialist workers, what the *Gardes mobiles* were for the bourgeois republicans, the Society of December 10 was for Bonaparte, the party fighting force peculiar to him. On his journeys the detachments of this society packing the railways had to improvise a public for him, stage public enthusiasm, roar *vive l'Empereur*, insult and thrash republicans, of course, under the protection of the police. On his return journeys to Paris they had to form the advance guard, forestall counter-demonstrations or disperse them. The Society of December 10 belonged to him, it was *his* work, his very own idea. Whatever else he appropriates is put into his hands by the force of circumstances; whatever else he does, the circumstances do for him or he is content to copy from the deeds of others. But Bonaparte with official phrases about order, religion, family and property in public, before the citizens, and with the secret society of the Schufterles and Spiegelbergs,[38] the society of disorder, prostitution and theft, behind him—that is Bonaparte himself as original author, and the history of the Society of December 10 is his own history.

Now it had happened by way of exception that people's representatives belonging to the party of Order came under the cudgels of the Decembrists. Still more, Yon, the Police Commissioner assigned to the National Assembly and charged with watching over its safety, acting on the deposition of a certain Alais, advised the Permanent Commission that a section of the Decembrists had decided to assassinate General Changarnier and Dupin, the President of the National Assembly, and had already designated the individuals who were to perpetrate the deed. One comprehends the terror of M. Dupin. A parliamentary enquiry into the Society of December 10, that is, the profanation of the Bonapartist secret world, seemed inevitable. Just before the meeting of the National Assembly Bonaparte providently disbanded his society, naturally only on paper, for in a detailed memoir at the end of 1851 Police Prefect Carlier still sought in vain to move him to really break up the Decembrists.

The Society of December 10 was to remain the private army of Bonaparte until he succeeded in transforming the public army into a Society of December 10. Bonaparte made the first attempt at this shortly after the adjournment of the National Assembly, and precisely with the money just wrested from it. As a fatalist, he lives in the conviction that there are certain higher powers which man, and the soldier in particular, cannot withstand. Among these powers he counts, first and foremost, cigars and champagne, cold poultry and garlic sausage. Accordingly, to begin with, he treats officers and non-commissioned officers in his Elysée apartments to cigars and champagne, to cold poultry and garlic sausage. On October 3 he repeats this manoeuvre with the mass of the troops at the St. Maur review, and on October 10 the same manoeuvre on a still larger scale at the Satory army parade. The Uncle remembered the campaigns of Alexander in Asia, the Nephew the triumphal marches of Bacchus in the same land. Alexander was a demigod, to be sure, but Bacchus was a god and moreover the tutelary deity of the Society of December 10.

After the review of October 3, the Permanent Commission summoned War Minister d'Hautpoul. He promised that these breaches of discipline should not recur. We know how on October 10 Bonaparte kept d'Hautpoul's word. As Commander-in-Chief of the Paris army, Changarnier had commanded at both reviews. He, at once a member of the Permanent Commission, chief of the National Guard, the "saviour" of January 29 and June 13, the "bulwark of society," the candidate of the party of Order for presidential honours, the suspected Monk of two monarchies, had hitherto never acknowledged himself as the subordinate of the War Minister, had always openly derided the republican Constitution and had pursued Bonaparte with an ambiguous lordly protection. Now he was consumed with zeal for discipline against the War Minister and for the Constitution against Bonaparte. While on October 10 a section of the cavalry raised the shout: *"Vive Napoléon! Vivent les saucissons!"** Changarnier arranged that at least the infantry marching past under the command of his friend Neumayer should preserve an icy silence. As a punishment, the War Minister relieved General Neumayer of his post in Paris at Bonaparte's instigation, on the pretext of appointing him commanding general of the fourteenth and fifteenth military divisions. Neumayer refused this exchange of posts and so had to resign. Changarnier, for his part, published an order of the day on November 2, in which he forbade the troops to in-

---

* "Hurrah for Napoleon! Hurrah for the sausages!"—*Ed.*

dulge in political outcries or demonstrations of any kind while under arms. The Elysée newspapers[39] attacked Changarnier; the papers of the party of Order attacked Bonaparte; the Permanent Commission held repeated secret sessions in which it was repeatedly proposed to declare the country in danger; the army seemed divided into two hostile camps, with two hostile general staffs, one in the Elysée, where Bonaparte resided, the other in the Tuileries, the quarters of Changarnier. It seemed that only the meeting of the National Assembly was needed to give the signal for battle. The French public judged this friction between Bonaparte and Changarnier like that English journalist who characterized it in the following words:

"The political housemaids of France are sweeping away the glow ing lava of the revolution with old brooms and wrangle with one another while they do their work."

Meanwhile, Bonaparte hastened to remove the War Minister, d'Hautpoul, to pack him off in all haste to Algiers and to appoint General Schramm War Minister in his place. On November 12, he sent to the National Assembly a message of American prolixity, overloaded with detail, redolent of order, desirous of reconciliation, constitutionally acquiescent, treating of all and sundry, but not of the *questions brûlantes** of the moment. As if in passing, he made the remark that according to the express provisions of the Constitution the President alone could dispose of the army. The message closed with the following words of great solemnity:

"*Above all things, France demands tranquillity. . . . But bound by an oath, I shall keep within the narrow limits that it has set for me. . . :* As far as I am concerned, elected by the people and owing my power to it alone, I shall always bow to its lawfully expressed will. Should you resolve at this session on a revision of the Constitution, a Constituent Assembly will regulate the position of the executive power. If not, then the people will solemnly pronounce its decision in 1852. But whatever the solutions of the future may be, let us come to an under-

---

* *Questions brûlantes*: Burning questions.—*Ed.*

standing, so that passion, surprise or violence may never decide the destiny of a great nation.... What occupies my attention, above all, is not who will rule France in 1852, but how to employ the time which remains at my disposal so that the intervening period may pass by without agitation or disturbance. I have opened my heart to you with sincerity; you will answer my frankness with your trust, my good endeavours with your cooperation, and God will do the rest."

The respectable, hypocritically moderate, virtuously commonplace language of the bourgeoisie reveals its deepest meaning in the mouth of the autocrat of the Society of December 10 and the picnic hero of St. Maur and Satory.

The burgraves of the party of Order did not delude themselves for a moment concerning the trust that this opening of the heart deserved. About oaths they had long been *blasé*; they numbered in their midst veterans and virtuosos of political perjury. Nor had they failed to hear the passage about the army. They observed with annoyance that in its discursive enumeration of lately enacted laws the message passed over the most important law, the electoral law, in studied silence, and, moreover, in the event of there being no revision of the Constitution, left the election of the President in 1852 to the people. The electoral law was the leaden ball chained to the feet of the party of Order, which prevented it from walking and so much the more from storming forward! Moreover, by the official disbandment of the Society of December 10 and the dismissal of the War Minister d'Hautpoul, Bonaparte had with his own hand sacrificed the scapegoats on the altar of the country. He had blunted the edge of the expected collision. Finally, the party of Order itself anxiously sought to avoid, to mitigate, to gloss over any decisive conflict with the executive power. For fear of losing their conquests over the revolution, they allowed their rival to carry off the fruits thereof. "Above all things, France demands tranquillity." This was what the party of Order had cried to the revolution since February,* this was what

---

* 1848.—*Ed.*

Bonaparte's message cried to the party of Order. "Above all things, France demands tranquillity." Bonaparte committed acts that aimed at usurpation, but the party of Order committed "unrest" if it raised a row about these acts and construed them hypochondriacally. The sausages of Satory were quiet as mice when no one spoke of them. "Above all things, France demands tranquillity." Bonaparte demanded, therefore, that he be left in peace to do as he liked and the parliamentary party was paralyzed by a double fear, by the fear of again evoking revolutionary unrest and by the fear of itself appearing as the instigator of unrest in the eyes of its own class, in the eyes of the bourgeoisie. Consequently, since France demanded tranquillity above all things, the party of Order dared not answer "war" after Bonaparte had talked "peace" in his message. The public, which had anticipated scenes of great scandal at the opening of the National Assembly, was cheated of its expectations. The opposition deputies, who demanded the submission of the Permanent Commission's minutes on the October events, were outvoted by the majority. On principle, all debates that might cause excitement were eschewed. The proceedings of the National Assembly during November and December 1850 were without interest.

At last, towards the end of December, guerilla warfare began over a number of prerogatives of parliament. The movement got bogged in petty squabbles regarding the prerogatives of the two powers, since the bourgeoisie had done away with the class struggle for the moment by abolishing universal suffrage.

A judgment for debt had been obtained from the court against Mauguin, one of the People's Representatives. In answer to the enquiry of the President of the Court, the Minister of Justice, Rouher, declared that a *capias* should be issued against the debtor without further ado. Mauguin was thus thrown into the debtors' jail. The National Assembly flared up when it learned of the assault. Not only did it order his immediate release, but it even had him fetched forcibly from Clichy the same evening. by its *greffier*.* In order, however, to confirm its faith in the sanctity of private property and with the idea at the back of its mind of opening, in case of need, an asylum for *Montagnards* who had become troublesome, it declared imprisonment of People's Representatives for debt permissible after previously obtaining its consent. It forgot to decree that the President might also be locked up for debt. It destroyed the last semblance of the immunity that enveloped the members of its own body.

It will be remembered that, acting on the information given by a certain Alais, Police Commissioner Yon had denounced a section of the Decembrists for planning the murder of Dupin and Changarnier. In reference to this, at the very first sitting the quaestors made the proposal that parliament should form a police force of its own, paid out of the private budget of the National Assembly and absolutely independent of the police prefect. The Minister of the Interior, Baroche, protested against this invasion of his domain. A miserable compromise on this matter was concluded, according to which, true, the police commissioner of the Assembly was to be paid out of its private budget and to be appointed and dismissed by its quaestors, but only after previous agreement with the Minister of the Interior. Meanwhile criminal proceedings had been taken by the government against Alais, and here it was easy to represent his information as a hoax and through the mouth of the public prosecutor to cast ridicule upon Dupin, Changarnier, Yon and the whole National Assembly. Thereupon, on December 29, Minister Baroche writes a letter to Dupin in which he demands Yon's dismissal. The Bureau of the National Assembly decides to retain Yon in his position, but the National Assembly, alarmed by its violence in the Mauguin affair and accustomed when it has ventured a

---

* *Greffier*: Clerk.—*Ed.*

blow at the executive power to receive two blows from it in return, does not sanction this decision. It dismisses Yon as a reward for his official zeal and robs itself of a parliamentary prerogative indispensable against a man who does not decide by night in order to execute by day, but who decides by day and executes by night.

We have seen how on great and striking occasions during the months of November and December the National Assembly avoided or quashed the struggle with the executive power. Now we see it compelled to take it up on the pettiest occasions. In the Mauguin affair it confirms the principle of imprisoning People's Representatives for debt, but reserves the right to have it applied only to representatives obnoxious to itself and wrangles over this infamous privilege with the Minister of Justice. Instead of availing itself of the alleged murder plot to decree an enquiry into the Society of December 10 and irredeemably unmasking Bonaparte before France and Europe in his true character of chief of the Paris *lumpenproletariat*, it lets the conflict be degraded to a point where the only issue between it and the Minister of the Interior is which of them has the authority to appoint and dismiss a police commissioner. Thus, during the whole of this period, we see the party of Order compelled by its equivocal position to dissipate and disintegrate its struggle with the executive power in petty jurisdictional squabbles, petty-foggery, legalistic hairsplitting, and delimitational disputes, and to make the most ridiculous matters of form the substance of its activity. It does not dare to take up the conflict at the moment when this has significance from the standpoint of principle, when the executive power has really exposed itself and the cause of the National Assembly would be the cause of the nation. By so doing it would give the nation its marching orders, and it fears nothing more than that the nation should move. On such occasions it accordingly rejects the motions of the *Montagne* and proceeds to the order of the day. The question at issue in its larger aspects having thus been dropped, the executive power calmly bides the time when it can again take up the same question on petty and insignificant occasions, when this is, so to speak, of only local parliamentary interest. Then the repressed rage of the party of Order breaks out, then it tears away the curtain from the coulisses, then it denounces the President, then it declares the republic in danger, but then, also, its fervour appears absurd and the occasion for the struggle seems a hypocritical pretext or altogether not worth fighting about. The parliamentary storm becomes a storm in a teacup, the fight becomes an intrigue, the conflict a scandal. While the revolutionary classes gloat with malicious joy over the humiliation of the National Assembly, for they are just as enthusiastic about the parliamentary prerogatives of this Assembly as the latter is about the public liberties, the bourgeoisie outside parliament does not understand how the bourgeoisie inside parliament can waste time over such petty squabbles and imperil tranquillity by such pitiful rivalries with the President. It becomes confused by a strategy that makes peace at the moment when all the world is expecting battles, and attacks at the moment when all the world believes peace has been made.

On December 20, Pascal Duprat interpellated the Minister of the Interior concerning the Gold Bars Lottery. This lottery was a "daughter of Elysium."[40] Bonaparte with his faithful followers had brought her into the world and Police Prefect Carlier had placed her under his official protection, although French law forbids all lotteries with the exception of raffles for charitable purposes. Seven million lottery tickets at a franc apiece, the profits ostensibly to be devoted to shipping Parisian vagabonds to California. On the one hand, golden dreams were to supplant the socialist dreams of the Paris proletariat; the seductive prospect of the first prize, the doctrinaire right to work. Naturally, the Paris workers did not recognize in the glitter of the California gold bars the inconspicuous francs that were enticed out of their pockets. In the main, however, the matter was nothing short of a downright swindle. The vagabonds who wanted to open California gold mines without troubling to leave Paris were Bonaparte himself and his debt-ridden Round Table. The three millions voted by the National Assembly had been squandered in riotous living; in one way or another the coffers had to be replenished. In vain had Bonaparte opened a national subscription for the building of so-called *cités ouvrières,** and figured at the head of the list himself with a considerable sum. The hardhearted bourgeois waited mistrustfully for him to pay up his share and since this, naturally, did not ensue, the speculation in socialist castles in the air fell straightway to the ground. The gold bars proved a better draw. Bonaparte & Co. were not content to pocket part of the excess of the seven millions over the bars to be allotted in prizes; they manufactured false lottery tickets; they issued ten, fifteen and even twenty tickets with the same number—a financial operation in the spirit of the Society of December 10! Here the National Assembly was confronted not with the fictitious President of the republic, but with Bonaparte in the flesh. Here it could catch him in the act, in conflict not with the Constitution but with the *Code pénal.* If on Duprat's interpellation it proceeded to the order of the day, this did not happen merely because Girardin's motion that it should declare itself *"satisfait"* reminded the party of Order of its own systematic corruption. The bourgeois and, above all, the bourgeois inflated into a statesman, supplements his practical meanness by theoretical extravagance. As a statesman he becomes, like the state power that confronts him, a higher being that can only be fought in a higher, consecrated fashion.

Bonaparte, who precisely because he was a Bohemian, a princely *lumpenproletarian,* had the advantage over a rascally bourgeois in that he could conduct the struggle

---

* *Cités ouvrières:* Workers' settlements.—*Ed.*

meanly, now saw, after the Assembly had itself guided him with its own hand across the slippery ground of the military banquets, the reviews, the Society of December 10, and, finally, the *Code pénal*, that the moment had come when he could pass from an apparent defensive to the offensive. The minor defeats meanwhile sustained by the Minister of Justice, the Minister of War, the Minister of the Navy and the Minister of Finance, through which the National Assembly signified its snarling displeasure, troubled him little. He not only prevented the ministers from resigning and thus recognizing the sovereignty of parliament over the executive power, but could now consummate what he had begun during the recess of the National Assembly: the severance of the military power from parliament, the *removal of Changarnier*.

An Elysée paper published an order of the day alleged to have been addressed during the month of May to the First Military Division, and therefore proceeding from Changarnier, in which the officers were recommended, in the event of an insurrection, to give no quarter to the traitors in their own ranks, but to shoot them immediately and refuse the National Assembly the troops, should it requisition them. On January 3, 1851, the Cabinet was interpellated concerning this order of the day. For the investigation of this matter it requests a breathing space, first of three months, then of a week, finally of only twenty-four hours. The Assembly insists on an immediate explanation. Changarnier rises and declares that there never was such an order of the day. He adds that he will always hasten to comply with the demands of the National Assembly and that in case of a clash it can count on him. It receives his declaration with indescribable applause and passes a vote of confidence in him. It abdicates, it decrees its own impotence and the omnipotence of the army by placing itself under the private protection of a general; but the general deceives himself when he puts at its command against Bonaparte a power that he only holds as a fief from the same Bonaparte and when, in his turn, he expects to be protected by this parliament, by his own protégé in need of protection. Changarnier, however, believes in the mysterious power with which the bourgeoisie has endowed him since January 29, 1849. He considers himself the third power, existing side by side with both the other state powers. He shares the fate of the rest of this epoch's heroes, or rather saints, whose greatness consists precisely in the biassed great opinion of them that their party creates in its own interests and who shrink to everyday figures as soon as circumstances call on them to perform miracles. Unbelief is, in general, the mortal enemy of these reputed heroes and real saints. Hence their majestically moral indignation at the dearth of enthusiasm displayed by wits and scoffers.

The same evening, the ministers were summoned to the Elysée; Bonaparte insists on the dismissal of Changarnier; five ministers refuse to sign it; the *Moniteur* announces a ministerial crisis, and the press of the party of Order threatens to form a parliamentary army under Changarnier's command. The party of Order had constitutional authority to take this step. It merely had to appoint Changarnier President of the National Assembly and requisition any number of troops it pleased for its protection. It could do so all the more safely as Changarnier still actually stood at the head of the army and the Paris National Guard and was only waiting to be requisitioned together with the army. The Bonapartist press did not as yet even dare to question the right of the National Assembly directly to requisition troops, a legal scruple that in the given circumstances did not promise any success. That the army would have obeyed the orders of the National Assembly is probable when one bears in mind that Bonaparte had to search all Paris for eight days in order, finally, to find two generals—Baraguay d'Hilliers and Saint-Jean d'Angely—who declared themselves ready to countersign Changarnier's dismissal. That the party of Order, however, would have found in its own ranks and in parliament the necessary number of votes for such a resolution is more than doubtful, when one considers that eight days later two hundred and eighty-six votes detached themselves from the party and that in December 1851, at the last hour for decision, the *Montagne* still rejected a similar proposal. Nevertheless, the burgraves might, perhaps, still have succeeded in spurring the mass of their party to a heroism that consisted in feeling themselves secure behind a forest of bayonets and accepting the services of an army that had deserted to their camp. Instead of this, on the evening of January 6, Messrs. the Burgraves betook themselves to the Elysée in order to make Bonaparte desist from dismissing Changarnier by using statesmanlike phrases and urging considerations of state. Whomever one seeks to persuade, one acknowledges as master of the situation. On January 12, Bonaparte, assured by this step, appoints a new ministry in which the leaders of the old ministry, Fould and Baroche, remain. Saint-Jean d'Angely becomes War Minister, the *Moniteur* publishes the decree dismissing Changarnier, and his command is divided between Baraguay d'Hilliers, who receives the First Army Division, and Perrot, who receives the National Guard. The bulwark of society has been discharged, and while this does not cause any tiles to fall from the roofs, quotations on the *bourse* are, on the other hand, going up.

By repulsing the army, which places itself in the person of Changarnier at its disposal, and so surrendering the army irrevocably to the President, the party of Order declares that the bourgeoisie has forfeited its vocation to rule. A parliamentary ministry no longer existed. Having now indeed lost its grip on the army and National Guard, what forcible means remained to it with which simultaneously to maintain the usurped authority of parliament over the people and its constitutional authority against the President? None. Only the appeal to forceless principles remained to it now, to principles that it had itself always interpreted merely as general rules, which one prescribes for others in order to be able to move all the more freely oneself. The dismissal of Changarnier and the falling of the military power into Bonaparte's hands closes the first part of the period we are considering, the period of struggle between the party of Order and the executive power. War between the two powers has now been openly declared, is openly waged, but only after the party of Order has lost both arms and soldiers. Without the ministry, without the army, without the people, without public opinion, after its Electoral Law of May 31 no longer the representative of the sovereign nation, *sans* eyes, *sans* ears, *sans* teeth, *sans* everything, the National Assembly had undergone a gradual transformation into an *ancient French Parliament*[41] that has to leave action to the government and content itself with growling remonstrances *post festum.**

The party of Order receives the new ministry with a storm of indignation. General Bedeau recalls to mind the mildness of the Permanent Commission during the recess, and the excessive consideration it had shown by waiving the publication of its minutes. The Minister of the Interior now himself insists on the publication of these minutes, which by this time have naturally become as dull as ditchwater, disclose no fresh facts and have not the slightest effect on the *blasé* public. Upon Rémusat's proposal the National Assembly retires into its bureaux and appoints a "Committee for Extraordinary Measures." Paris departs the less from the rut of its everyday routine, since at this moment trade is prosperous, manufactories are busy, corn prices low, foodstuffs overflowing and the savings banks receive fresh deposits daily. The "extraordinary measures" that parliament has announced with so much noise fizzle out on January 18 in a no-confidence vote against the min-

---

* *Post festum*: After the feast, that is, belatedly.—*Ed.*

istry without General Changarnier even being mentioned. The party of Order had been forced to frame its motion in this way in order to secure the votes of the republicans, as, of all the measures of the ministry, Changarnier's dismissal is precisely the only one which the republicans approve of, while the party of Order is in fact not in a position to censure the other ministerial acts, which it had itself dictated.

The no-confidence vote of January 18 was passed by four hundred and fifteen votes to two hundred and eighty-six. Thus, it was carried only by a *coalition* of the extreme Legitimists and Orleanists with the pure republicans and the *Montagne*. Thus it proved that the party of Order had lost in conflicts with Bonaparte not only the ministry, not only the army, but also its independent parliamentary majority, that a squad of representatives had deserted from its camp, out of fanaticism for conciliation, out of fear of the struggle, out of lassitude, out of family regard for the state salaries so near and dear to them, out of speculation on ministerial posts becoming vacant (Odilon Barrot), out of sheer egoism, which makes the ordinary bourgeois always inclined to sacrifice the general interest of his class for this or that private motive. From the first, the Bonapartist representatives adhered to the party of Order only in the struggle against revolution. The leader of the Catholic party, Montalembert, had already at that time thrown his influence into the Bonapartist scale, since he despaired of the parliamentary party's prospects of life. Lastly, the leaders of this party, Thiers and Berryer, the Orleanist and the Legitimist, were compelled openly to proclaim themselves republicans, to confess that their hearts were royalist but their heads republican, that the parliamentary republic was the sole possible form for the rule of the bourgeoisie as a whole. Thus they were compelled, before the eyes of the bourgeois class itself, to stigmatize the Restoration plans, which they continued indefatigably to pursue behind parliament's back as an intrigue as dangerous as it was brainless.

The no-confidence vote of January 18 hit the ministers and not the President. But it was not the ministry, it was the President who had dismissed Changarnier. Should the party of Order impeach Bonaparte himself? On account of his restoration desires? The latter merely supplemented their own. On account of his conspiracy in connection with the military reviews and the Society of December 10? They had buried these themes long since under simple orders of the day. On account of the dismissal of the hero of January 29 and June 13, the man who in May 1850 threatened to set fire to all four corners of Paris in the event of a rising? Their allies of the *Montagne* and Cavaignac did not even allow them to raise the fallen bulwark of society by means of an official attestation of sympathy. They themselves could not deny the President the constitutional authority to dismiss a general. They only raged because he made an unparliamentary use of his constitutional right. Had they not continually made an unconstitutional use of their parliamentary prerogative, particularly in regard to the abolition of universal suffrage? They were therefore reduced to moving within strictly parliamentary limits. And it took that peculiar malady which since 1848 has raged all over the Continent, *parliamentary cretinism,* which holds those infected by it fast in an imaginary world and robs them of all sense, all memory, all understanding of the rude external world—it took this parliamentary cretinism for those who had destroyed all the conditions of parliamentary power with their own hands, and were bound to destroy them in their struggle with the other classes, still to regard their parliamentary victories as victories and to believe they hit the President by striking at his ministers. They merely gave him the opportunity to humiliate the National Assembly afresh in the eyes of the nation. On January 20 the *Moniteur* announced that the resignation of the entire ministry had been accepted. On the pretext that no parliamentary party any longer had a majority, as the vote of January 18, this fruit of the coalition between *Montagne* and royalists, proved, and pending the formation of a new majority, Bonaparte appointed a so-called transition ministry, not one member of which was a member of parliament, all being absolutely unknown and insignificant individuals, a ministry of mere clerks and copyists. The party of Order could now work to exhaustion playing with these marionettes; the executive power no longer thought it worth while to be seriously represented in the National Assembly. The more his ministers were pure dummies, the more manifestly Bonaparte concentrated the whole executive power in his own person and the more scope he had to exploit it for his own ends.

In coalition with the *Montagne*, the party of Order revenged itself by rejecting the grant to the President of one million eight hundred thousand francs, which the chief of the Society of December 10 had compelled his ministerial clerks to propose. This time a majority of only a hundred and two votes decided the matter; thus twenty-seven fresh votes had fallen away since January 18; the dissolution of the party of Order was making progress. At the same time, in order that there might not for a moment be any mistake about the meaning of its coalition with the *Montagne*, it scorned even to consider a proposal signed by a hundred and eighty-nine members of the *Montagne* calling for a general amnesty of political offenders. It sufficed for the Minister of the Interior, a certain Vaïsse, to declare that the tranquillity was only apparent, that in secret great agitation prevailed, that in secret ubiquitous societies were being organized, the democratic papers were preparing to come out again, the reports from the Departments were unfavourable, the Geneva refugees were directing a conspiracy spreading by way of Lyons over all the south of France, France was on the verge of an industrial and commercial crisis, the manufacturers of Roubaix had reduced working hours, that the prisoners of Belle Isle[42] were in revolt—it sufficed for even a mere Vaïsse to conjure up the red spectre and the party of Order rejected without discussion a motion that would certainly have won the National Assembly immense popularity and thrown Bonaparte back into its arms. Instead of letting itself be intimidated by the executive power with the prospect of fresh disturbances, it ought rather to have allowed the class struggle a little elbowroom, so as to keep the executive power dependent on itself. But it did not feel equal to the task of playing with fire.

Meanwhile, the so-called transition ministry continued to vegetate until the middle of April. Bonaparte wearied and befooled the National Assembly with continual new ministerial combinations. Now he seemed to want to form a republican ministry with Lamartine and Billault, now a parliamentary one with the inevitable Odilon Barrot, whose name may never be missing when a dupe is necessary, then a Legitimist ministry with Vatimesnil and Benoit d'Azy, and then again an Orleanist one with Maleville. While he thus kept the different factions of the party of Order in tension against one another and alarmed them as a whole by the prospect of a republican ministry and the consequent inevitable restoration of universal suffrage, he at the same time engendered in the bourgeoisie the conviction that his honest efforts to form a parliamentary ministry were being frustrated by the irreconcilability of the royalist factions. The bourgeoisie, however, cried out all the louder for a "strong government"; it found it all the more unpardonable to leave France "without administration," the more a general commercial crisis seemed now to be approaching and won recruits for Socialism in the towns just as the ruinously low price of corn did in the countryside. Trade became daily slacker, the unemployed hands increased perceptibly, ten thousand workers, at least, were breadless in Paris, innumerable factories stood idle in Rouen, Mulhouse, Lyons, Roubaix, Tourcoing, St.

Etienne, Elbeuf, etc. Under these circumstances Bonaparte could venture, on April 11, to restore the ministry of January 18: Messers. Rouher, Fould, Baroche, etc., reinforced by M. Léon Faucher, whom the Constituent Assembly during its last days had, with the exception of five votes cast by ministers, unanimously stigmatized by a vote of no-confidence for sending out false telegrams. The National Assembly had therefore gained a victory over the ministry on January 18, had struggled with Bonaparte for three months, only to have Fould and Baroche on April 11 admit the puritan Faucher as a third party into their ministerial alliance.

In November 1849, Bonaparte had contented himself with an *unparliamentary* ministry, in January 1851 with an *extra-parliamentary* one, and on April 11 he felt strong enough to form an *anti-parliamentary* ministry, which harmoniously combined in itself the no-confidence votes of both Assemblies, the Constituent and the Legislative, the republican and the royalist. This gradation of ministries was the thermometer with which parliament could measure the decrease of its own vital heat. By the end of April the latter had fallen so low that Persigny, in a personal interview, could urge Changarnier to go over to the camp of the President. Bonaparte, he assured him, regarded the influence of the National Assembly as completely destroyed, and the proclamation was already prepared that was to be published after the *coup d'état*, which was kept steadily in view but was by chance again postponed. Changarnier informed the leaders of the party of Order of the obituary notice, but who believes that bedbug bites are fatal? And parliament, stricken, disintegrated and death-tainted as it was, could not prevail upon itself to see in its duel with the grotesque chief of the Society of December 10 anything but a duel with a bedbug. But Bonaparte answered the party of Order as Agesilaus did King Agis:

"*I seem to thee an ant, but one day I shall be a lion.*"[43]

VI

The coalition with the *Montagne* and the pure republicans, to which the party of Order saw itself condemned in its unavailing efforts to maintain possession of the military power and to reconquer supreme control of the executive power, proved incontrovertibly that it had forfeited its independent *parliamentary majority.* On May 28, the mere power of the calendar, of the hour hand of the clock, gave the signal for its complete disintegration. With May 28, the last year of the life of the National Assembly began. It had now to decide for continuing the Constitution unaltered or for revising it. But revision of the Constitution, that implied not only rule of the bourgeoisie or of the petty-bourgeois democracy, democracy or proletarian anarchy, parliamentary republic or Bonaparte, it implied at the same time Orleans or Bourbon! Thus fell in the midst of parliament the apple of discord that was bound to inflame openly the conflict of interests which split the party of Order into hostile factions. The party of Order was a combination of heterogeneous social substances. The question of revision generated a political temperature at which the product again decomposed into its original constituents.

The interest of the Bonapartists in a revision was simple. For them it was above all a question of abolishing Article 45, which forbade Bonaparte's re-election and the prolongation of his authority. No less simple appeared the position of the republicans. They unconditionally rejected any revision; they saw in it a universal conspiracy against the republic. Since they commanded *more than a quarter of the votes* in the National Assembly and, according to the Constitution, three-quarters of the votes were required for a resolution for revision to be legally valid and for the convocation of a revising Assembly, they only needed to count their votes to be sure of victory. And they were sure of victory.

As against these clear positions, the party of Order found itself caught in inextricable contradictions. If it should reject revision, it would imperil the *status quo*, since it would leave Bonaparte only one way out, that of force, and since on the second Sunday in May 1852, at the decisive moment, it would be surrendering France to revolutionary anarchy, with a President who had lost his authority, with a parliament which for a long time had not possessed it and with a people that meant to reconquer it. If it voted for constitutional revision, it knew that it voted in vain and would be bound to fail constitutionally because of the veto of the republicans. If it unconstitutionally declared a simple majority vote to be binding, then it could hope to dominate the revolution only if it subordinated itself unconditionally to the sovereignty of the executive power, then it would make Bonaparte master of the Constitution, of its revision and of itself. Only a partial revision which would prolong the authority of the President would pave the way for imperial usurpation. A general revision which would shorten the existence of the republic would bring the dynastic claims into unavoidable conflict, for the conditions of a Bourbon and the conditions of an Orleanist Restoration were not only different, they were mutually exclusive.

The parliamentary republic was more than the neutral territory on which the two factions of the French bourgeoisie, Legitimists and Orleanists, large landed property and industry, could dwell side by side with equality of rights. It was the unavoidable condition of their *common* rule, the sole form of state in which their general class interest subjected to itself at the same time both the claims of their particular factions and all the remaining classes of society. As royalists they fell back into their old antagonism, into the struggle for the supremacy of landed property or of money, and the highest expression of this antagonism, its personification, was their kings themselves, their dynasties. Hence the resistance of the party of Order to the *recall of the Bourbons.*

The Orleanist and people's representative Creton had in 1849, 1850 and 1851 periodically introduced a motion for the revocation of the decree exiling the royal families. Just as regularly parliament presented the spectacle of an Assembly of royalists that obdurately barred the gates through which their exiled kings might return home. Richard III had murdered Henry VI, remarking that he was too good for this world and belonged in heaven. They declared France too bad to possess her kings again. Constrained by force of circumstances, they had become republicans and repeatedly sanctioned the popular decision that banished their kings from France.

A revision of the Constitution—and circumstances compelled taking it into consideration—called in question, along with the republic, the common rule of the two bourgeois factions, and revived, with the possibility of a monarchy, the rivalry of the interests which it had predominantly represented by turns, the struggle for the supremacy of one faction over the other. The diplomats of the party of Order believed they could settle the struggle by an amalgamation of the two dynasties, by a so-called *fusion* of the royalist parties and their royal houses. The real fusion of the Restoration and the July Monarchy was the parliamentary republic, in which Orleanist and Legitimist colours were obliterated and the various species of bourgeois disappeared in the bourgeois as such, in the bourgeois genus. Now, however, Orleanist was to become Legitimist and Legitimist Orleanist. Royalty, in which their antagonism was personified, was to embody their

97

unity; the expression of their exclusive factional interests was to become the expression of their common class interest; the monarchy was to do that which only the abolition of two monarchies, the republic, could do and had done. This was the philosopher's stone, to produce which the doctors of the party of Order racked their brains. As if the Legitimist monarchy could ever become the monarchy of the industrial bourgeois or the bourgeois monarchy ever become the monarchy of the hereditary landed aristocracy. As if landed property and industry could fraternize under *one* crown, when the crown could only descend to one head, the head of the elder brother or of the younger. As if industry could come to terms with landed property at all, so long as landed property does not decide itself to become industrial. If Henry V should die tomorrow, the Count of Paris would not on that account become the king of the Legitimists unless he ceased to be the king of the Orleanists. The philosophers of fusion, however, who became more vociferous in proportion as the question of revision came to the fore, who had provided themselves with an official daily organ in the *Assemblée Nationale*[44] and who are again at work even at this very moment (February 1852), considered the whole difficulty to be due to the opposition and rivalry of the two dynasties. The attempts to reconcile the Orleans family with Henry V, begun since the death of Louis Philippe, but, like the dynastic intrigues generally, played at only while the National Assembly was in recess, during the *entr'actes*, behind the scenes, sentimental coquetry with the old superstition rather than seriously-meant business, now became grand performances of state, enacted by the party of Order on the public stage, instead of in amateur theatricals, as hitherto. The couriers sped from Paris to Venice,[45] from Venice to Claremont, from Claremont to Paris. The Count of Chambord issues a manifesto in which "with the help of all the members of his family" he announces not his, but the "national" Restoration. The Orleanist Salvandy throws himself at the feet of Henry V. The Legitimist chiefs, Berryer, Benoit d'Azy, Saint-Priest, travel to Claremont in order to persuade the Orleans set, but in vain. The fusionists perceive too late that the interests of the two bourgeois factions neither lose exclusiveness nor gain pliancy when they become accentuated in the form of family interests, the interests of two royal houses. If Henry V were to recognize the Count of Paris as his successor—the sole success that the fusion could achieve at best—the House of Orleans would not win any claim that the childlessness of Henry V had not already secured to it, but it would lose all claims that it had gained through the July Revolution. It would waive its original claims, all the titles that it had wrested from the older branch of the Bourbons in almost a hundred years of struggle; it would barter away its historical prerogative, the prerogative of the modern kingdom, for the prerogative of its genealogical tree. The fusion, therefore, would be nothing but a voluntary abdication of the House of Orleans, its resignation to Legitimacy, repentant withdrawal from the Protestant state church into the Catholic. A withdrawal, moreover, that would not even bring it to the throne which it had lost, but to the throne's steps, on which it had been born. The old Orleanist ministers, Guizot, Duchâtel, etc., who likewise hastened to Claremont to advocate the fusion, in fact represented merely the *Katzenjammer** over the July Revolution, the despair felt in regard to the bourgeois kingdom and the kingliness of the bourgeois, the superstitious belief in Legitimacy as the last charm against anarchy. Imagining themselves mediators between Orleans and Bourbons, they were in reality merely Orleanist renegades, and the prince of Joinville received them as such. On the other hand, the viable, bellicose section of the Orleanists, Thiers, Baze, etc., convinced Louis Philippe's family all the more easily that if any directly monarchist restoration presupposed the fusion of the two

---

* *Katzenjammer*: The "morning-after" feeling.—*Ed.*

dynasties and if any such fusion, however, presupposed abdication of the House of Orleans, it was, on the contrary, wholly in accord with the tradition of their forefathers to recognize the republic for the moment and wait until events permitted the conversion of the presidential chair into a throne. Rumours of Joinville's candidature were circulated, public curiosity was kept in suspense and, a few months later, in September, after the rejection of revision, his candidature was publicly proclaimed.

The attempt at a royalist fusion of Orleanists with Legitimists had thus not only failed; it had destroyed their *parliamentary fusion*, their common republican form, and had broken up the party of Order into its original component parts; but the more the estrangement between Claremont and Venice grew, the more their settlement broke down and the Joinville agitation gained ground, so much the more eager and earnest became the negotiations between Bonaparte's minister Faucher and the Legitimists.

The disintegration of the party of Order did not stop at its original elements. Each of the two great factions, in its turn, underwent decomposition anew. It was as if all the old nuances that had formerly fought and jostled one another within each of the two circles, whether Legitimist or Orleanist, had thawed out again like dry Infusoria on contact with water, as if they had acquired anew sufficient vital energy to form groups of their own and independent antagonisms. The Legitimists dreamed that they were back among the controversies between the Tuileries and the Pavillon Marsan, between Villèle and Polignac.[46] The Orleanists relived the golden days of the tourneys between Guizot, Molé, Broglie, Thiers and Odilon Barrot.

That part of the party of Order which was eager for revision, but was divided again on the limits to revision, a section composed of the Legitimists led by Berryer and Falloux, on the one hand, and by La Rochejaquelein, on the other, and of the conflict-weary Orleanists led by Molé, Broglie, Montalembert and Odilon Barrot, agreed with the

Bonapartist representatives on the following indefinite and broadly framed motion:

"With the object of restoring to the nation the full exercise of its sovereignty, the undersigned Representatives move that the Constitution be revised."

At the same time, however, they unanimously declared through their reporter Tocqueville that the National Assembly had not the right to move the *abolition of the republic*, that this right was vested solely in the Revising Chamber. For the rest, the Constitution might be revised only in a *"legal"* manner, hence only if the constitutionally prescribed three-quarters of the number of votes were cast in favour of revision. On July 19, after six days of stormy debate, revision was rejected, as was to be anticipated. Four hundred and forty-six votes were cast for it, but two hundred and seventy-eight against. The extreme Orleanists, Thiers, Changarnier, etc., voted with the republicans and the *Montagne*.

Thus the majority of parliament declared against the Constitution, but this Constitution itself declared for the minority and that its vote was binding. But had not the party of Order subordinated the Constitution to the parliamentary majority on May 31, 1850, and on June 13, 1849? Up to now, was not its whole policy based on the subordination of the paragraphs of the Constitution to the decisions of the parliamentary majority? Had it not left to the democrats the antediluvian superstitious belief in the letter of the law, and castigated the democrats for it? At the present moment, however, revision of the Constitution meant nothing but continuation of the presidential authority, just as continuation of the Constitution meant nothing but Bonaparte's deposition. Parliament had declared for him, but the Constitution declared against parliament. He therefore acted in the sense of parliament when he tore up the Constitution and he acted in the sense of the Constitution when he dispersed parliament.

Parliament had declared the Constitution and, with the latter, its own rule to be "beyond the majority"; by its vote it had abolished the Constitution and prolonged the term of presidential power, while declaring at the same time that neither can the one die nor the other live so long as it itself continues to exist. Those who were to bury it were standing at the door. While it debated on revision, Bonaparte removed General Baraguay d'Hilliers, who had proved irresolute, from the command of the First Army Division and appointed in his place General Magnan, the victor of Lyons, the hero of the December days, one of his creatures, who under Louis Philippe had already compromised himself more or less in Bonaparte's favour on the occasion of the Boulogne expedition.

The party of Order proved by its decision on revision that it knew neither how to rule nor how to serve; neither how to live nor how to die; neither how to suffer the republic nor how to overthrow it; neither how to uphold the Constitution nor how to throw it overboard; neither how to cooperate with the President nor how to break with him. To whom, then, did it look for the solution of all the contradictions? To the calendar, to the course of events. It ceased to presume to sway the events. It therefore challenged the events to assume sway over it, and thereby challenged the power to which in the struggle against the people it had surrendered one attribute after another until it itself stood impotent before this power. In order that the head of the executive power might be able the more undisturbedly to draw up his plan of campaign against it, strengthen his means of attack, select his tools and fortify his positions, it resolved precisely at this critical moment to retire from the stage and adjourn for three months, from August 10 to November 4.

The parliamentary party was not only dissolved into its two great factions, each of these factions was not only split up within itself, but the party of Order in parliament had fallen out with the party of Order *outside* parliament.

The spokesmen and scribes of the bourgeoisie, its platform and its press, in short, the ideologists of the bourgeoisie and the bourgeoisie itself, the representatives and the represented, faced one another in estrangement and no longer understood one another.

The Legitimists in the provinces, with their limited horizon and their unlimited enthusiasm, accused their parliamentary leaders, Berryer and Falloux, of deserting to the Bonapartist camp and of defection from Henry V. Their *fleur-de-lis* minds believed in the fall of man, but not in diplomacy.

Far more fateful and decisive was the breach of the commercial bourgeoisie with its politicians. It reproached them, not as the Legitimists reproached theirs, with having abandoned their principles, but, on the contrary, with clinging to principles that had become useless.

I have already indicated above that since Fould's entry into the ministry the section of the commercial bourgeoisie which had held the lion's share of power under Louis Philippe, namely, the *aristocracy of finance*, had become Bonapartist. Fould represented not only Bonaparte's interests in the *bourse,* he represented at the same time the interests of the *bourse* before Bonaparte. The position of the aristocracy of finance is most strikingly depicted in a passage from its European organ, the London *Economist.* In its number of February 1, 1851, its Paris correspondent writes:

"Now we have it stated from numerous quarters that above all things France demands tranquillity. The President declares it in his message to the Legislative Assembly; it is echoed from the tribune; it is asserted in the journals; it is announced from the pulpit; *it is demonstrated by the sensitiveness of the public funds at the least prospect of disturbance, and their firmness the instant it is made manifest that the executive is victorious.*"

In its issue of November 29, 1851, *The Economist* declares in its own name:

"*The President is the guardian of order, and is now recognized as such on every Stock Exchange of Europe*"

The aristocracy of finance, therefore, condemned the parliamentary struggle of the party of Order with the executive power as a *disturbance of order*, and celebrated every victory of the President over its ostensible representatives as a *victory of order*. By the aristocracy of finance must here be understood not merely the great loan promoters and speculators in public funds, in regard to whom it is immediately obvious that their interests coincide with the interests of the state power. All modern finance, the whole of the banking business, is interwoven in the closest fashion with public credit. A part of their business capital is necessarily invested and put out at interest in quickly convertible public funds. Their deposits, the capital placed at their disposal and distributed by them among merchants and industrialists, are partly derived from the dividends of holders of government securities. If in every epoch the stability of the state power signified Moses and the prophets to the entire money market and to the priests of this money market, why not all the more so today, when every deluge threatens to sweep away the old states, and the old state debts with them?

The *industrial bourgeoisie*, too, in its fanaticism for order, was angered by the squabbles of the parliamentary party of Order with the executive power. After their vote of January 18 on the occasion of Changarnier's dismissal, Thiers, Anglès, Sainte-Beuve, etc., received from their constituents, in precisely the industrial districts, public reproofs in which particularly their coalition with the *Montagne* was scourged as high treason to order. If, as we have seen, the boastful taunts, the petty intrigues which marked the struggle of the party of Order with the President merited no better reception, then, on the other hand, this bourgeois party, which required its representatives to allow the military power to pass from its own parliament to an adventurous pretender without offering resistance, was not even worth the intrigues that were squandered in its interests. It proved that the struggle to maintain its *public* interests, its own *class interests,* its *political power*, only troubled and upset it, as it was a disturbance of private business.

With barely an exception, the bourgeois dignitaries of the Departmental towns, the municipal authorities, the judges of the Commercial Courts, etc., everywhere received Bonaparte on his tours in the most servile manner, even when, as in Dijon, he made an unrestrained attack on the National Assembly, and especially on the party of Order.

When trade was good, as it still was at the beginning of 1851, the commercial bourgeoisie raged against any parliamentary struggle, lest trade be put out of humour. When trade was bad, as it continually was from the end of February 1851, the commercial bourgeoisie accused the parliamentary struggles of being the cause of stagnation and cried out for them to stop in order that trade might start again. The revision debates came on just in this bad period. Since the question here was whether the existing form of state was to be or not to be, the bourgeoisie felt itself all the more justified in demanding from its Representatives the ending of this torturous provisional arrangement and at the same time the maintenance of the *status quo.* There was no contradiction in this. By the end of the provisional arrangement it understood precisely its continuation, the postponement to a distant future of the moment when a decision had to be reached. The *status quo* could be maintained in only two ways: prolongation of Bonaparte's authority or his constitutional retirement and the election of Cavaignac. A section of the bourgeoisie desired the latter solution and knew no better advice to give its Representatives than to keep silent and leave the burning question untouched. They were of the opinion that if their Representatives did not speak, Bonaparte would not act. They wanted an ostrich parliament that would hide its head in order to remain unseen. Another section of the bourgeoisie desired, because Bonaparte was already in the presidential chair, to leave him sitting in it, so that everything might remain in the same old rut. They were indignant because their parliament did not openly infringe the Constitution and abdicate without ceremony.

The General Councils of the Departments, those provincial representative bodies of the big bourgeoisie, which met from August 25 on during the recess of the National Assembly, declared almost unanimously for revision, and thus against parliament and in favour of Bonaparte.

Still more unequivocally than in its falling out with its *parliamentary representatives* the bourgeoisie displayed its wrath against its literary representatives, its own press. The sentences to ruinous fines and shameless terms of imprisonment, on the verdicts of bourgeois juries, for every attack of bourgeois journalists on Bonaparte's usurpationist desires, for every attempt of the press to defend the political rights of the bourgeoisie against the executive power, astonished not merely France, but all Europe.

While the *parliamentary party of Order*, by its clamour for tranquillity, as I have shown, committed itself to quiescence, while it declared the political rule of the bourgeoisie to be incompatible with the safety and existence of the bourgeoisie, by destroying with its own hands in the struggle against the other classes of society all the conditions for its own regime, the parliamentary regime, the *extra-parliamentary mass of the bourgeoisie*, on the other hand, by its servility towards the President, by its vilification of parliament, by its brutal maltreatment of its own press, invited Bonaparte to suppress and annihilate its speaking and writing section, its politicians and its *literati*, its platform and its press, in order that it might then be able to pursue its private affairs with full confidence in the protection of a strong and unrestricted government. It declared unequivocally that it longed to get rid of its own political rule in order to get rid of the troubles and dangers of ruling.

And this extra-parliamentary bourgeoisie, which had already rebelled against the purely parliamentary and literary struggle for the rule of its own class and betrayed the leaders of this struggle, now dares after the event to indict the proletariat for not having risen in a bloody struggle, a life-and-death struggle on its behalf! This bourgeoisie, which every moment sacrificed its general class interests, that is, its political interests, to the narrowest and most sordid private interests, and demanded a similar sacrifice from its Representatives, now moans that the proletariat has sacrificed its [the bourgeoisie's] ideal political interests to its [the proletariat's] material interests. It poses as a lovely being that has been misunderstood and deserted in the decisive hour by the proletariat misled by Socialists. And it finds a general echo in the bourgeois world. Naturally, I do not speak here of German shyster politicians and riffraff of the same persuasion. I refer, for example, to the already quoted *Economist*, which as late as November 29, 1851, that is, four days prior to the *coup d'état*, had declared Bonaparte to be the "guardian of order," but the Thiers and Berryers to be "anarchists," and on December 27, 1851, after Bonaparte had quieted these anarchists, is already vociferous concerning the treason to "the skill, knowledge, discipline, mental influence, intellectual resources and moral weight of the middle and upper ranks" committed by the masses of "ignorant, untrained, and stupid *proletaires*." The stupid, ignorant and vulgar mass was none other than the bourgeois mass itself.

In the year 1851, France, to be sure, had passed through a kind of minor trade crisis. The end of February showed a decline in exports compared with 1850; in March trade suffered and factories closed down; in April the position of the industrial Departments appeared as desperate as after the February days; in May business had still not revived; as late as June 28 the holdings of the Bank of France showed, by the enormous growth of deposits and the equally great decrease in advances on bills of exchange, that production was at a standstill, and it was not until the middle of October that a progressive improvement of business again set in. The French bourgeoisie attributed this trade stagnation to purely political causes, to the struggle between parliament and the executive power, to the precariousness of a merely provisional form of state, to the terrifying prospect of the second Sunday in May 1852. I will not deny that all these circumstances had a depressing effect on some branches of industry in Paris and the Departments. But in any case this influence of the political conditions was only local and inconsiderable. Does this require further proof than the fact that the improvement of trade set in towards the middle of October, at the very moment when the political situation grew worse, the political horizon darkened and a thunderbolt from Elysium was expected at any moment? For the rest, the French bourgeois, whose "skill, knowledge, spiritual insight and intellectual resources" reach no further than his nose, could throughout the period of the Industrial Exhibition in London[47] have found the cause of his commercial misery right under his nose. While in France factories were closed down, in England commercial bankruptcies broke out. While in April and May the industrial panic reached a climax in France, in April and May the commercial panic reached a climax in England. Like the French woollen industry, so the English woollen industry suffered, and as French silk manufacture, so did English silk manufacture. True, the English cotton mills continued working, but no longer at the same profits as in 1849 and 1850. The only difference was that the crisis in France was industrial, in England commercial; that while in France the factories stood idle, in England they extended operations, but under less favourable conditions than in preceding years; that in France it was exports, in England imports which were hardest hit. The common cause, which is naturally not to be sought within the bounds of the

French political horizon, was obvious. The years 1849 and 1850 were years of the greatest material prosperity and of an overproduction that appeared as such only in 1851. At the beginning of this year it was given a further special impetus by the prospect of the Industrial Exhibition. In addition there were the following special circumstances: first, the partial failure of the cotton crop in 1850 and 1851, then the certainty of a bigger cotton crop than had been expected; first the rise, then the sudden fall, in short, the fluctuations in the price of cotton. The crop of raw silk, in France at least, had turned out to be even below the average yield. Woollen manufacture, finally, had expanded so much since 1848 that the production of wool could not keep pace with it and the price of raw wool rose out of all proportion to the price of woollen manufactures. Here, then, in the raw material of three industries for the world market, we have already threefold material for a stagnation in trade. Apart from these special circumstances, the apparent crisis of 1851 was nothing else but the halt which over-production and over-speculation invariably make in describing the industrial cycle, before they summon all their strength in order to rush feverishly through the final phase of this cycle and arrive once more at their starting-point, the *general trade crisis*. During such intervals in the history of trade, commercial bankruptcies break out in England, while in France industry itself is reduced to idleness, being partly forced into retreat by the competition, just then becoming intolerable, of the English in all markets, and being partly singled out for attack as a luxury industry by every business stagnation. Thus, besides the general crisis, France goes through national trade crises of her own, which are nevertheless determined and conditioned far more by the general state of the world market than by French local influences. It will not be without interest to contrast the judgment of the English bourgeois with the prejudice of the French bourgeois. In its annual trade report for 1851, one of the largest Liverpool houses writes:

"Few years have more thoroughly belied the anticipations formed at their commencement than the one just closed; instead of the great prosperity which was almost unanimously looked for it has proved one of the most discouraging that has been seen for the last quarter of a century—this, of course, refers to the mercantile, not to the manufacturing classes. And yet there certainly were grounds for anticipating the reverse at the beginning of the year—stocks of produce were moderate, money was abundant, and food was cheap, a plentiful harvest well secured, unbroken peace on the Continent, and no political or fiscal disturbances at home; indeed, the wings of commerce were never more unfettered.... To what source, then, is this disastrous result to be attributed? We believe to *over-trading* both in imports and exports. Unless our merchants will put more stringent limits to their freedom of action, nothing but a *triennial* panic can keep us in check."[48]

Now picture to yourself the French bourgeois, how in the throes of this business panic his trade-crazy brain is tortured, set in a whirl and stunned by rumours of *coups d'état* and the restoration of universal suffrage, by the struggle between parliament and the executive power, by the Fronde war between Orleanists and Legitimists, by the communist conspiracies in the south of France, by alleged *Jacqueries* in the Departments of Nièvre and Cher, by the advertisements of the different candidates for the presidency, by the cheapjack solutions offered by the journals, by the threats of the republicans to uphold the Constitution and universal suffrage by force of arms, by the gospel-preaching émigré heroes *in partibus*, who announced that the world would come to an end on the second Sunday in May 1852—think of all this and you will comprehend why in this unspeakable, deafening chaos of fusion, revision, prorogation, constitution, conspiration, coalition, emigration, usurpation and revolution, the bourgeois madly snorts at his parliamentary republic: "*Rather an end with terror than terror without end!*"

Bonaparte understood this cry. His power of comprehension was sharpened by the growing turbulence of creditors who, with each sunset which brought settling day, the second Sunday in May 1852, nearer, saw a movement of the stars protesting their earthly bills of exchange. They had become veritable astrologers. The National Assembly had blighted Bonaparte's hopes of a constitutional prolongation of his authority; the candidature of the Prince of Joinville forbade further vacillation.

If ever an event has, well in advance of its coming, cast its shadow before, it was Bonaparte's *coup d'état*. As early as January 29, 1849, barely a month after his election, he had made a proposal about it to Changarnier. In the summer of 1849 his own Prime Minister, Odilon Barrot, had covertly denounced the policy of *coups d'état*; in the winter of 1850 Thiers had openly done so. In May 1851, Persigny had sought once more to win Changarnier for the *coup*; the *Messager de l'Assemblée*[49] had published an account of these negotiations. During every parliamentary storm, the Bonapartist journals threatened a *coup d'état*, and the nearer the crisis drew, the louder grew their tone. In the orgies that Bonaparte kept up every night with men and women of the "swell mob," as soon as the hour of midnight approached and copious potations had loosened tongues and fired imaginations, the *coup d'état* was fixed for the following morning. Swords were drawn, glasses clinked, the Representatives were thrown out of the window, the imperial mantle fell upon Bonaparte's shoulders, until the following morning banished the spook once more and astonished Paris learned, from vestals of little reticence and from indiscreet paladins, of the danger it had once again escaped. During the months of September and October rumours of a *coup d'état* followed fast one after the other. Simultaneously, the shadow took on colour, like a variegated daguerreotype. Look up the September and October copies of the organs of the European daily press and you will find, word for word, intimations like the following: "Paris is full of rumours of a *coup d'état*. The capital is to be filled with troops during the night, and the next morning is to bring decrees which will dissolve the National Assembly, declare the Department of the Seine in a state of siege, restore universal suffrage and appeal to the people. Bonaparte is said to be seeking ministers for the execution of these illegal decrees." The letters that bring these tidings always end with the fateful word *"postponed."* The *coup d'état* was ever the fixed idea of Bonaparte. With this idea he had again set foot on French soil. He was so obsessed by it that he continually betrayed it and blurted it out. He was so weak that, just as continually, he gave it up again. The shadow of the *coup d'état* had become so familiar to the Parisians as a spectre that they were not willing to believe in it when it finally appeared in the flesh. What allowed the *coup d'état* to succeed was, therefore, neither the reticent reserve of the chief of the Society of December 10 nor the fact that the National Assembly was caught unawares. If it succeeded, it succeeded despite *his* indiscretion and with *its* foreknowledge, a necessary, inevitable result of antecedent developments.

On October 10 Bonaparte announced to his ministers his decision to restore universal suffrage; on the sixteenth they handed in their resignations; on the twenty-sixth Paris learned of the formation of the Thorigny ministry. Police Prefect Carlier was simultaneously replaced by Maupas; the head of the First Military Division, Magnan, concentrated the most reliable regiments in the capital. On November 4, the National Assembly resumed its sittings. It had nothing better to do than to recapitulate in a short, succinct form the course it had gone through and to prove that it was buried only after it had died.

The first post that it forfeited in the struggle with the executive power was the ministry. It had solemnly to admit this loss by accepting at full value the Thorigny ministry, a mere shadow cabinet. The Permanent Commission had received M. Giraud with laughter when he presented himself in the name of the new ministers. Such a weak ministry for such strong measures as the restoration of universal suffrage! Yet the precise object was to get nothing through *in* parliament, but everything *against* parliament.

On the very first day of its re-opening, the National Assembly received the message from Bonaparte in which he demanded the restoration of universal suffrage and the abolition of the law of May 31, 1850. The same day his ministers introduced a decree to this effect. The National Assembly at once rejected the ministry's motion of urgency and rejected the law itself on November 13 by three hundred and fifty-five votes to three hundred and forty-eight. Thus, it tore up its mandate once more; it once more confirmed the fact that it had transformed itself from the freely elected representatives of the people into the usurpatory parliament of a class; it acknowledged once more that it had itself cut in two the muscles which connected the parliamentary head with the body of the nation.

If by its motion to restore universal suffrage the executive power appealed from the National Assembly to the people, the legislative power appealed by its Quaestors' Bill from the people to the army. This Quaestors' Bill was to establish its right of directly requisitioning troops, of forming a parliamentary army. While it thus designated the army as the arbitrator between itself and the people, between itself and Bonaparte, while it recognized the army as the decisive state power, it had to confirm, on the other hand, the fact that it had long given up its claim to dominate this power. By debating its right to requisition troops, instead of requisitioning them at once, it betrayed its doubts about its own powers. By rejecting the Quaestors' Bill, it made public confession of its impotence. This bill was defeated, its proponents lacking 108 votes of a majority. The *Montagne* thus decided the issue. It found itself in the position of Buridan's ass, not, indeed, between two bundles of hay with the problem of deciding which was the more attractive, but between two showers of blows with the problem of deciding which was the harder. On the one hand, there was the fear of Changarnier; on the other, the fear of Bonaparte. It must be confessed that the position was no heroic one.

On November 18, an amendment was moved to the law on municipal elections introduced by the party of Order, to the effect that instead of three years', one year's domicile should suffice for municipal electors. The amendment was lost by a single vote, but this one vote immediately proved to be a mistake. By splitting up into its hostile factions, the party of Order had long ago forfeited its independent parliamentary majority. It showed now that there was no longer any majority at all in parliament. The National Assembly had become *incapable of transacting business*. Its atomic constituents were no longer held together by any force of cohesion; it had drawn its last breath; it was dead.

Finally, a few days before the catastrophe, the extraparliamentary mass of the bourgeoisie was solemnly to confirm once more its breach with the bourgeoisie in parliament. Thiers, as a parliamentary hero infected more than the rest with the incurable disease of parliamentary cretinism, had, after the death of parliament, hatched out, together with the Council of State, a new parliamentary intrigue, a Responsibility Law by which the President was to be firmly held within the limits of the Constitution. Just as, on laying the foundation stone of the new market halls in Paris on September 15, Bonaparte, like a second Masaniello, had enchanted the *dames des halles*, the fishwives —to be sure, one fishwife outweighed seventeen burgraves in real power; just as after the introduction of the Quaestors' Bill he enraptured the lieutenants he regaled in the Elysée, so now, on November 25, he swept off their feet the industrial bourgeoisie, which had gathered at the circus to receive at his hands prize medals for the London Industrial Exhibition. I shall give the significant portion of his speech as reported in the *Journal des Débats*:

"With such unhoped-for successes, I am justified in reiterating how great the French republic would be if it were permitted to pursue its real interests and reform its institutions, instead of being constantly disturbed by demagogues, on the one hand, and by monarchist hallucinations, on the other. (Loud, stormy and repeated applause from every part of the amphitheatre.) The monarchist hallucinations hinder all progress and all important branches of industry. In place of progress nothing but struggle. One sees men who were formerly the most zealous supporters of the royal authority and prerogative become partisans of a Convention merely in order to weaken the authority that has sprung from universal suffrage. (Loud and repeated applause.) We see men who have suffered most from the Revolution, and have deplored it most, provoke a new one, and merely in order to fetter the nation's will. ... I promise you tranquillity for the future, etc., etc. (Bravo, bravo, a storm of bravos)."

Thus the industrial bourgeoisie applauds with servile bravos the *coup d'état* of December 2, the annihilation of parliament, the downfall of its own rule, the dictatorship of Bonaparte. The thunder of applause on November 25 had its answer in the thunder of cannon on December 4, and it was on the house of Monsieur Sallandrouze, who had clapped most, that they clapped most of the bombs.

Cromwell, when he dissolved the Long Parliament, went alone into its midst, drew out his watch in order that it should not continue to exist a minute after the time limit fixed by him, and drove out each one of the members of parliament with hilariously humourous taunts. Napoleon, smaller than his prototype, at least betook himself on the eighteenth Brumaire to the legislative body and read out to it, though in a faltering voice, its sentence of death. The second Bonaparte, who, moreover, found himself in possession of an executive power very different from that of Cromwell or Napoleon, sought his model not in the annals of world history, but in the annals of the Society of December 10, in the annals of the criminal courts. He robs the Bank of France of twenty-five million francs, buys General Magnan with a million, the soldiers with fifteen francs apiece and liquor, comes together with his accomplices secretly like a thief in the night, has the houses of the most dangerous parliamentary leaders broken into and Cavaignac, Lamoricière, Le Flô, Changarnier, Charras, Thiers, Baze, etc., dragged from their beds and put in prison, the chief squares of Paris and the parliamentary building occupied by troops, and cheap-Jack placards posted early in the morning on all the walls, proclaiming the dissolution of the National Assembly and the Council of State, the restoration of universal suffrage and the placing of the Seine Department in a state of siege. In like manner, he inserted a little later in the *Moniteur* a false document which asserted that influential parliamentarians had grouped themselves round him and formed a state *consulta.*

The rump parliament, assembled in the *mairie* building of the tenth *arrondissement* and consisting mainly of Legitimists and Orleanists, votes the deposition of Bonaparte amid repeated cries of "Long live the Republic," unavailingly harangues the gaping crowds before the building and is finally led off in the custody of African sharpshooters, first to the d'Orsay barracks, and later packed into prison vans and transported to the prisons of Mazas, Ham and Vincennes. Thus ended the party of Order, the Legislative Assembly and the February Revolution. Before hastening to close, let us briefly summarize the latter's history:

I. *First period.* From February 24 to May 4, 1848. February period. Prologue. Universal brotherhood swindle.

II. *Second period.* Period of constituting the republic and of the Constituent National Assembly.

1. May 4 to June 25, 1848. Struggle of all classes against the proletariat. Defeat of the proletariat in the June days.

2. June 25 to December 10, 1848. Dictatorship of the pure bourgeois republicans. Drafting of the Constitution. Proclamation of a state of siege in Paris. The bourgeois dictatorship set aside on December 10 by the election of Bonaparte as President.

3. December 20, 1848 to May 28, 1849. Struggle of the Constituent Assembly with Bonaparte and with the party of Order in alliance with him. Passing of the Constituent Assembly. Fall of the republican bourgeoisie.

III. *Third period.* Period of the *constitutional republic* and of the *Legislative National Assembly.*

1. May 28, 1849 to June 13, 1849. Struggle of the petty bourgeoisie with the bourgeoisie and with Bonaparte. Defeat of the petty-bourgeois democracy.

2. June 13, 1849 to May 31, 1850. Parliamentary dictatorship of the party of Order. It completes its rule by abolishing universal suffrage, but loses the parliamentary ministry.

3. May 31, 1850 to December 2, 1851. Struggle between the parliamentary bourgeoisie and Bonaparte.

(a) May 31, 1850 to January 12, 1851. Parliament loses the supreme command of the army.

(b) January 12 to April 11, 1851. It is worsted in its attempts to regain the administrative power. The party of Order loses its independent parliamentary majority. Its coalition with the republicans and the *Montagne.*

(c) April 11, 1851 to October 9, 1851. Attempts at revision, fusion, prorogation. The party of Order decomposes into its separate constituents. The breach between the bourgeois parliament and press and the mass of the bourgeoisie becomes definite.

(d) October 9 to December 2, 1851. Open breach between parliament and the executive power. Parliament performs its dying act and succumbs, left in the lurch by its own class, by the army and by all the remaining classes. Passing of the parliamentary regime and of bourgeois rule. Victory of Bonaparte. Parody of restoration of empire.

VII

On the threshold of the February Revolution, the *social republic* appeared as a phrase, as a prophecy. In the June days of 1848, it was drowned in the blood of the *Paris proletariat*, but it haunts the subsequent acts of the drama like a ghost. The *democratic republic* announces its arrival. On June 13, 1849, it is dissipated together with its *petty bourgeois*, who have taken to their heels, but in its flight it blows its own trumpet with redoubled boastfulness. The *parliamentary republic*, together with the bourgeoisie, takes possession of the entire stage; it enjoys its existence to the full, but December 2, 1851 buries it to the accompaniment of the anguished cry of the royalists in coalition: "Long live the Republic!"

The French bourgeoisie balked at the domination of the working proletariat; it has brought the *lumpenproletariat* to domination, with the chief of the Society of December 10 at the head. The bourgeoisie kept France in breathless fear of the future terrors of red anarchy; Bonaparte discounted this future for it when, on December 4, he had the eminent bourgeois of the Boulevard Montmartre and the Boulevard des Italiens shot down at their windows by the liquor-inspired army of order. It apotheosized the sword; the sword rules it. It destroyed the revolutionary press; its own press has been destroyed. It placed popular meetings under police supervision; its salons are under the supervision of the police. It disbanded the democratic National Guards; its own National Guard is disbanded. It imposed a state of siege; a state of siege is imposed upon it. It supplanted the juries by military commissions; its juries are supplanted by military commissions. It subjected public education to the sway of the priests; the priests subject it to their own education. It transported people without trial; it is being transported without trial. It repressed every stirring in society by means of the state power; every stirring in its society is suppressed by means of the state power. Out of enthusiasm for its purse, it rebelled against its own politicians and men of letters; its politicians and men of letters are swept aside, but its purse is being plundered now that its mouth has been gagged and its pen broken. The bourgeoisie never wearied of crying out to the revolution what Saint Arsenius cried out to the Christians: *"Fuge, tace, quiesce!* Flee, be silent, keep still!" Bonaparte cries to the bourgeoisie: *"Fuge, tace, quiesce!* Flee, be silent, keep still!"

The French bourgeoisie had long ago found the solution to Napoleon's dilemma: *"Dans cinquante ans l'Europe sera républicaine ou cosaque."** It had found the solution to it in the *"république cosaque."*** No Circe, by means of black magic, has distorted that work of art, the bourgeois republic, into a monstrous shape. That republic has lost nothing but the semblance of respectability. Present-day France*** was contained in a finished state within the parliamentary republic. It only required a bayonet thrust for the bubble to burst and the monster to spring forth before our eyes.

Why did the Paris proletariat not rise in revolt after December 2?

The overthrow of the bourgeoisie had as yet been only decreed; the decree had not been carried out. Any serious insurrection of the proletariat would at once have put fresh

---

* "In fifty years Europe will be republican or Cossack."—*Ed.*
** "Cossack republic."—*Ed.*
*** I.e., France after the *coup d'état* of December 2, 1851.—*Ed.*

life into the bourgeoisie, would have reconciled it with the army and ensured a second June defeat for the workers.

On December 4 the proletariat was incited by bourgeois and *épicier* to fight. On the evening of that day several legions of the National Guard promised to appear, armed and uniformed, on the scene of battle. For the bourgeois and the *épicier* had got wind of the fact that in one of his decrees of December 2 Bonaparte abolished the secret ballot and enjoined them to record their "yes" or "no" in the official registers after their names. The resistance of December 4 intimidated Bonaparte. During the night he caused placards to be posted on all the street corners of Paris, announcing the restoration of the secret ballot. The bourgeois and the *épicier* believed that they had gained their end. Those who failed to appear next morning were the bourgeois and the *épicier*.

By a *coup de main* during the night of December 1 to 2, Bonaparte had robbed the Paris proletariat of its leaders, the barricade commanders. An army without officers, averse to fighting under the banner of the *Montagnards* because of the memories of June 1848 and 1849 and May 1850, it left to its vanguard, the secret societies, the task of saving the insurrectionary honour of Paris, which the bourgeoisie had so unresistingly surrendered to the soldiery that, later on, Bonaparte could sneeringly give as his motive for disarming the National Guard—his fear that its arms would be turned against it itself by the anarchists!

"C'est le triomphe complet et définitif du socialisme!"* Thus Guizot characterized December 2. But if the overthrow of the parliamentary republic contains within itself the germ of the triumph of the proletarian revolution, its immediate and palpable result was *the victory of Bonaparte over parliament, of the executive power over the legislative power, of force without phrases over the force*

---

* "This is the complete and final triumph of Socialism!"—*Ed.*

of phrases. In parliament the nation made its general will the law, that is, it made the law of the ruling class its general will. Before the executive power it renounces all will of its own and submits to the superior command of an alien will, to authority. The executive power, in contrast to the legislative power, expresses the heteronomy of a nation, in contrast to its autonomy. France, therefore, seems to have escaped the despotism of a class only to fall back beneath the despotism of an individual, and, what is more, beneath the authority of an individual without authority. The struggle seems to be settled in such a way that all classes, equally impotent and equally mute, fall on their knees before the rifle butt.

But the revolution is thoroughgoing. It is still journeying through purgatory. It does its work methodically. By December 2, 1851, it had completed one half of its preparatory work; it is now completing the other half. First it perfected the parliamentary power, in order to be able to overthrow it. Now that it has attained this, it perfects the *executive power*, reduces it to its purest expression, isolates it, sets it up against itself as the sole target, in order to concentrate all its forces of destruction against it. And when it has done this second half of its preliminary work, Europe will leap from its seat and exultantly exclaim: Well grubbed, old mole![50]

This executive power with its enormous bureaucratic and military organization, with its ingenious state machinery, embracing wide strata, with a host of officials numbering half a million, besides an army of another half million, this appalling parasitic body, which enmeshes the body of French society like a net and chokes all its pores, sprang up in the days of the absolute monarchy, with the decay of the feudal system, which it helped to hasten. The seignorial privileges of the landowners and towns became transformed into so many attributes of the state power, the feudal dignitaries into paid officials and the motley pattern of conflicting medieval plenary powers into the regulated plan of a state authority whose work is divided and centralized as in a factory. The first French Revolution, with its task of breaking all separate local, territorial, urban and provincial powers in order to create the civil unity of the nation, was bound to develop what the absolute monarchy had begun: centralization, but at the same time the extent, the attributes and the agents of governmental power. Napoleon perfected this state machinery. The Legitimist Monarchy and the July Monarchy added nothing but a greater division of labour, growing in the same measure as the division of labour within bourgeois society created new groups of interests, and, therefore, new material for state administration. Every *common* interest was straightway severed from society, counterposed to it as a higher, *general* interest, snatched from the activity of society's members themselves and made an object of government activity, from a bridge, a schoolhouse and the communal property of a village community to the railways, the national wealth and the national university of France. Finally, in its struggle against the revolution, the parliamentary republic found itself compelled to strengthen, along with the repressive measures, the resources and centralization of governmental power. All revolutions perfected this machine instead of smashing it. The parties that contended in turn for domination regarded the possession of this huge state edifice as the principal spoils of the victor.

But under the absolute monarchy, during the first Revolution, under Napoleon, bureaucracy was only the means of preparing the class rule of the bourgeoisie. Under the Restoration, under Louis Philippe, under the parliamentary republic, it was the instrument of the ruling class, however much it strove for power of its own.

Only under the second Bonaparte does the state seem to have made itself completely independent. As against civil society, the state machine has consolidated its position so thoroughly that the chief of the Society of December 10 suffices for its head, an adventurer blown in from abroad, raised on the shield by a drunken soldiery, which he has bought with liquor and sausages, and which he must continually ply with sausage anew. Hence the downcast despair, the feeling of most dreadful humiliation and degradation that oppresses the breast of France and makes her catch her breath. She feels dishonoured.

And yet the state power is not suspended in midair. Bonaparte represents a class, and the most numerous class of French society at that, the *small-holding [Parzellen] peasants.*

Just as the Bourbons were the dynasty of big landed property and just as the Orleans were the dynasty of money, so the Bonapartes are the dynasty of the peasants, that is, the mass of the French people. Not the Bonaparte who submitted to the bourgeois parliament, but the Bonaparte who dispersed the bourgeois parliament is the chosen of the peasantry. For three years the towns had succeeded in falsifying the meaning of the election of December 10 and in cheating the peasants out of the restoration of the empire. The election of December 10, 1848, has been consummated only by the *coup d'état* of December 2, 1851.

The small-holding peasants form a vast mass, the members of which live in similar conditions but without entering into manifold relations with one another. Their mode of production isolates them from one another instead of bringing them into mutual intercourse. The isolation is increased by France's bad means of communication and by the poverty of the peasants. Their field of production, the small holding, admits of no division of labour in its cultivation, no application of science and, therefore, no diversity of development, no variety of talent, no wealth of social relationships. Each individual peasant family is almost self-sufficient; it itself directly produces the major part of its consumption and thus acquires its means of life more through exchange with nature than in intercourse with society. A small holding, a peasant and his family; alongside them another small holding, another peasant and another family. A few score of these make up a village, and a few score of villages make up a Department. In this way, the great mass of the French nation is formed by simple addition of homologous magnitudes, much as potatoes in a sack form a sack of potatoes. In so far as millions of families live under economic conditions of existence that separate their mode of life, their interests and their culture from those of the other classes, and put them in hostile opposition to the latter, they form a class. In so far as there is merely a local interconnection among these small-holding peasants, and the identity of their interests begets no community, no national bond and no political organization among them, they do not form a class. They are consequently incapable of enforcing their class interest in their own name, whether through a parliament or through a convention. They cannot represent themselves, they must be represented. Their representative must at the same time appear as their master, as an authority over them, as an unlimited governmental power that protects them against the other classes and sends them rain and sunshine from above. The political influence of the small-holding peasants, therefore, finds its final expression in the executive power subordinating society to itself.

Historical tradition gave rise to the belief of the French peasants in the miracle that a man named Napoleon would bring all the glory back to them. And an individual turned up who gives himself out as the man because he bears the name of Napoleon, in consequence of the *Code Napoléon*,[51] which lays down that *la recherche de la paternité est interdite.** After a vagabondage of twenty years and after a series of grotesque adventures, the legend finds fulfilment and the man becomes Emperor of the French. The fixed idea of the Nephew was realized, because it coincided

---

* Enquiry into paternity is forbidden.—*Ed.*

with the fixed idea of the most numerous class of the French people.

But, it may be objected, what about the peasant risings in half of France, the raids on the peasants by the army, the mass incarceration and transportation of peasants?

Since Louis XIV, France has experienced no similar persecution of the peasants "on account of demagogic practices."

But let there be no misunderstanding. The Bonaparte dynasty represents not the revolutionary, but the conservative peasant; not the peasant that strikes out beyond the condition of his social existence, the small holding, but rather the peasant who wants to consolidate this holding, not the country folk who, linked up with the towns, want to overthrow the old order through their own energies, but on the contrary those who, in stupefied seclusion within this old order, want to see themselves and their small holdings saved and favoured by the ghost of the empire. It represents not the enlightenment, but the superstition of the peasant; not his judgment, but his prejudice; not his future, but his past; not his modern Cevennes, but his modern Vendée.[52]

The three years' rigorous rule of the parliamentary republic had freed a part of the French peasants from the Napoleonic illusion and had revolutionized them, even if only superficially; but the bourgeoisie violently repressed them, as often as they set themselves in motion. Under the parliamentary republic the modern and the traditional consciousness of the French peasant contended for mastery. This progress took the form of an incessant struggle between the schoolmasters and the priests. The bourgeoisie struck down the schoolmasters. For the first time the peasants made efforts to behave independently in the face of the activity of the government. This was shown in the continual conflict between the *maires* and the prefects. The bourgeoisie deposed the *maires*. Finally, during the period of the parliamentary republic, the peasants of different localities rose against their own offspring, the army. The bourgeoisie punished them with states of siege and punitive expeditions. And this same bourgeoisie now cries out about the stupidity of the masses, the vile multitude, that has betrayed it to Bonaparte. It has itself forcibly strengthened the empire sentiments [*Imperialismus*] of the peasant class, it conserved the conditions that form the birthplace of this peasant religion. The bourgeoisie, to be sure, is bound to fear the stupidity of the masses as long as they remain conservative, and the insight of the masses as soon as they become revolutionary.

In the risings after the *coup d'état*, a part of the French peasants protested, arms in hand, against their own vote of December 10, 1848. The school they had gone through since 1848 had sharpened their wits. But they had made themselves over to the underworld of history; history held them to their word, and the majority was still so prejudiced that in precisely the reddest Departments the peasant population voted openly for Bonaparte. In its view, the National Assembly had hindered his progress. He had now merely broken the fetters that the towns had imposed on the will of the countryside. In some parts the peasants even entertained the grotesque notion of a convention side by side with Napoleon.

After the first revolution had transformed the peasants from semi-villeins into freeholders, Napoleon confirmed and regulated the conditions on which they could exploit undisturbed the soil of France which had only just fallen to their lot and slake their youthful passion for property. But what is now causing the ruin of the French peasant is his small holding itself, the division of the land, the form of property which Napoleon consolidated in France. It is precisely the material conditions which made the feudal peasant a small-holding peasant and Napoleon an emperor. Two generations have sufficed to produce the inevitable result: progressive deterioration of agriculture, progressive indebtedness of the agriculturist. The "Napoleonic" form of property, which at the beginning of the nineteenth century was the condition for the liberation and enrichment of the French country folk, has developed in the course of this century into the law of their enslavement and pauperization. And precisely this law is the first of the *"idées napoléoniennes"* which the second Bonaparte has to uphold. If he still shares with the peasants the illusion that the cause of their ruin is to be sought, not in this smallholding property itself, but outside it, in the influence of secondary circumstances, his experiments will burst like soap bubbles when they come in contact with the relations of production.

The economic development of small-holding property has radically changed the relation of the peasants to the other classes of society. Under Napoleon, the fragmentation of the land in the countryside supplemented free competition and the beginning of big industry in the towns. The peasant class was the ubiquitous protest against the landed aristocracy which had just been overthrown. The roots that small-holding property struck in French soil deprived feudalism of all nutriment. Its landmarks formed the natural fortifications of the bourgeoisie against any surprise attack on the part of its old overlords. But in the course of the nineteenth century the feudal lords were replaced by urban usurers; the feudal obligation that went with the land was replaced by the mortgage; aristocratic landed property was replaced by bourgeois capital. The small holding of the peasant is now only the pretext that allows the capitalist to draw profits, interest and rent from the soil, while leaving it to the tiller of the soil himself to see how he can extract his wages. The mortgage debt burdening the soil of France imposes on the French peasantry payment of an amount of interest equal to the annual interest on the entire British national debt. Small-holding property, in this enslavement by capital to which its development inevitably pushes forward, has transformed the mass of the French nation into troglodytes. Sixteen million peasants (including women and children) dwell in hovels, a large number of which have but one opening, others only two and the most favoured only three. And windows are to a house what the five senses are to the head. The bourgeois order, which at the beginning of the century set the state to stand guard over the newly arisen small holding and manured it with laurels, has become a vampire that sucks out its blood and brains and throws it into the alchemistic cauldron of capital. The *Code Napoléon* is now nothing but a *codex* of distraints, forced sales and compulsory auctions. To the four million (including children, etc.) officially recognized paupers, vagabonds, criminals and prostitutes in France must be added five million who hover on the margin of existence and either have their haunts in the countryside itself or, with their rags and their children, continually desert the countryside for the towns and the towns for the countryside. The interests of the peasants, therefore, are no longer, as under Napoleon, in accord with, but in opposition to the interests of the bourgeoisie, to capital. Hence the peasants find their natural ally and leader in the *urban proletariat*, whose task is the overthrow of the bourgeois order. But *strong and unlimited government*—and this is the second "*idée napoléonienne*," which the second Napoleon has to carry out—is called upon to defend this "material" order by force. This "*ordre matériel*" also serves as the catchword in all of Bonaparte's proclamations against the rebellious peasants.

Besides the mortgage which capital imposes on it, the small holding is burdened by *taxes*. Taxes are the source of life for the bureaucracy, the army, the priests and the court, in short, for the whole apparatus of the executive power. Strong government and heavy taxes are identical. By its very nature, small-holding property forms a suitable basis for an all-powerful and innumerable bureaucracy. It creates a uniform level of relationships and persons over the whole surface of the land. Hence it also permits

of uniform action from a supreme centre on all points of
this uniform mass. It annihilates the aristocratic interme-
diate grades between the mass of the people and the state
power. On all sides, therefore, it calls forth the direct in-
terference of this state power and the interposition of its
immediate organs. Finally, it produces an unemployed
surplus population for which there is no place either on the
land or in the towns, and which accordingly reaches out
for state offices as a sort of respectable alms, and provokes
the creation of state posts. By the new markets which
he opened at the point of the bayonet, by the plundering
of the Continent, Napoleon repaid the compulsory taxes
with interest. These taxes were a spur to the industry of
the peasant, whereas now they rob his industry of its last
resources and complete his inability to resist pauperism.
And an enormous bureaucracy, well-gallooned and well-
fed, is the *"idée napoléonienne"* which is most congenial
of all to the second Bonaparte. How could it be otherwise,
seeing that alongside the actual classes of society he is
forced to create an artificial caste, for which the maintenance of his regime becomes a bread-and-butter question?
Accordingly, one of his first financial operations was the
raising of officials' salaries to their old level and the creation of new sinecures.

Another *"idée napoléonienne"* is the domination of the
priests as an instrument of government. But while in its
accord with society, in its dependence on natural forces
and its submission to the authority which protected it from
above, the small holding that had newly come into being
was naturally religious, the small holding that is ruined
by debts, at odds with society and authority, and driven
beyond its own limitations naturally becomes irreligious.
Heaven was quite a pleasing accession to the narrow
strip of land just won, more particularly as it makes the
weather; it becomes an insult as soon as it is thrust forward as substitute for the small holding. The priest then
appears as only the anointed bloodhound of the earthly

129

police—another *"idée napolé*nienne.*"* On the next occasion, the expedition against Rome will take place in France itself, but in a sense opposite to that of M. de Montalembert.

Lastly, the culminating point of the *"idées napoléoniennes"* is the preponderance of the *army.* The army was the *point d'honneur** of the small-holding peasants, it was they themselves transformed into heroes, defending their new possessions against the outer world, glorifying their recently won nationhood, plundering and revolutionizing the world. The uniform was their own state dress; war was their poetry; the small holding, extended and rounded off in imagination, was their fatherland, and patriotism the ideal form of the sense of property. But the enemies against whom the French peasant has now to defend his property are not the Cossacks; they are the *huissiers*** and the tax collectors. The small holding lies no longer in the so-called fatherland, but in the register of mortgages. The army itself is no longer the flower of the peasant youth; it is the swamp-flower of the peasant *lumpenproletariat.* It consists in large measure of *remplaçants*, of substitutes, just as the second Bonaparte is himself only a *remplaçant,* the substitute for Napoleon. It now performs its deeds of valour by hounding the peasants in masses like chamois, by doing *gendarme* duty, and if the internal contradictions of his system chase the chief of the Society of December 10 over the French border, his army, after some acts of brigandage, will reap, not laurels, but thrashings.

One sees: *all* "idées napoléoniennes" *are ideas of the undeveloped small holding in the freshness of its youth*; for the small holding that has outlived its day they are an absurdity. They are only the hallucinations of its death struggle, words that are transformed into phrases, spirits transformed into ghosts. But the parody of the empire [*des*

---

* Matter of honour, a point of special touch.—*Ed.*
** *Huissiers:* Bailiffs.—*Ed.*

Imperialismus] was necessary to free the mass of the French nation from the weight of tradition and to work out in pure form the opposition between the state power and society. With the progressive undermining of small-holding property, the state structure erected upon it collapses. The centralization of the state that modern society requires arises only on the ruins of the military-bureaucratic government machinery which was forged in opposition to feudalism.[53]

The condition of the French peasants provides us with the answer to the riddle of the *general elections of December 20 and 21,* which bore the second Bonaparte up Mount Sinai, not to receive laws, but to give them.

Manifestly, the bourgeoisie had now no choice but to elect Bonaparte. When the puritans at the Council of Constance[54] complained of the dissolute lives of the popes and wailed about the necessity of moral reform, Cardinal Pierre d'Ailly thundered at them: "Only the devil in person can still save the Catholic Church, and you ask for angels." In like manner, after the *coup d'état,* the French bourgeoisie cried: Only the chief of the Society of December 10 can still save bourgeois society! Only theft can still save property; only perjury, religion; bastardy, the family; disorder, order!

As the executive authority which has made itself an independent power, Bonaparte feels it to be his mission to safeguard "bourgeois order." But the strength of this bourgeois order lies in the middle class. He looks on himself, therefore, as the representative of the middle class and issues decrees in this sense. Nevertheless, he is somebody solely due to the fact that he has broken the political power of this middle class and daily breaks it anew. Consequently, he looks on himself as the adversary of the political and literary power of the middle class. But by protecting its material power, he generates its political power anew. The cause must accordingly be kept alive; but the effect, where it manifests itself, must be done away with. But this cannot pass off without slight confusions of cause and effect, since in their interaction both lose their distinguishing features. New decrees that obliterate the border line. As against the bourgeoisie, Bonaparte looks on himself, at the same time, as the representative of the peasants and of the people in general, who wants to make the lower classes of the people happy within the frame of bourgeois society. New decrees that cheat the "True Socialists"[55] of their statecraft in advance. But, above all, Bonaparte looks on himself as the chief of the Society of December 10, as the representative of the *lumpenproletariat* to which he himself, his *entourage*, his government and his army belong, and whose prime consideration is to benefit itself and draw California lottery prizes from the state treasury. And he vindicates his position as chief of the Society of December 10 with decrees, without decrees and despite decrees.

This contradictory task of the man explains the contradictions of his government, the confused groping about which seeks now to win, now to humiliate first one class and then another and arrays all of them uniformly against him, whose practical uncertainty forms a highly comical contrast to the imperious, categorical style of the government decrees, a style which is faithfully copied from the Uncle.

Industry and trade, hence the business affairs of the middle class, are to prosper in hothouse fashion under the strong government. The grant of innumerable railway concessions. But the Bonapartist *lumpenproletariat* is to enrich itself. The initiated play *tripotage** on the *bourse* with the railway concessions. But no capital is forthcoming for the railways. Obligation of the Bank to make advances on railway shares. But, at the same time, the Bank is to be exploited for personal ends and therefore must be cajoled. Release of the Bank from the obligation to publish its re-

---

* *Tripotage*: Hanky-panky.—*Ed.*

port weekly. Leonine agreement of the Bank with the government. The people are to be given employment. Initiation of public works. But the public works increase the obligations of the people in respect of taxes. Hence reduction of the taxes by an onslaught on the *rentiers*, by conversion of the five per cent bonds to four-and-a-half per cent. But, once more, the middle class must receive a *douceur.** Therefore doubling of the wine tax for the people, who buy it *en détail,*** and halving of the wine tax for the middle class, who drink it *en gros.**** Dissolution of the actual workers' associations, but promises of miracles of association in the future. The peasants are to be helped. Mortgage banks that expedite their getting into debt and accelerate the concentration of property. But these banks are to be used to make money out of the confiscated estates of the House of Orleans. No capitalist wants to agree to this condition, which is not in the decree, and the mortgage bank remains a mere decree, etc., etc.

Bonaparte would like to appear as the patriarchal benefactor of all classes. But he cannot give to one class without taking from another. Just as at the time of the Fronde it was said of the Duke of Guise that he was the most *obligeant* man in France because he had turned all his estates into his partisans' obligations to him, so Bonaparte would fain be the most *obligeant* man in France and turn all the property, all the labour of France into a personal obligation to himself. He would like to steal the whole of France in order to be able to make a present of her to France or, rather, in order to be able to buy France anew with French money, for as the chief of the Society of December 10 he must needs buy what ought to belong to him. And all the state institutions, the Senate, the Council of State, the legislative body, the Legion of Honour, the soldiers' medals, the washhouses, the public works,

* *Douceur*: Sop.—*Ed.*
** *En détail*: By retail.—*Ed.*
*** *En gros*: Wholesale.—*Ed.*

the railways, the *état major** of the National Guard to the exclusion of privates, and the confiscated estates of the House of Orleans—all become parts of the institution of purchase. Every place in the army and in the government machine becomes a means of purchase. But the most important feature of this process, whereby France is taken in order to give to her, is the percentages that find their way into the pockets of the head and the members of the Society of December 10 during the turnover. The witticism with which Countess L., the mistress of M. de Morny, characterized the confiscation of the Orleans estates: *"C'est le premier vol*** de l'aigle"**** is applicable to every flight of this *eagle*, which is more like a *raven*. He himself and his adherents call out to one another daily like that Italian Carthusian admonishing the miser who, with boastful display, counted up the goods on which he could yet live for years to come: *"Tu fai conto sopra i beni, bisogna prima far il conto sopra gli anni."***** Lest they make a mistake in the years, they count the minutes. A bunch of blokes push their way forward to the court, into the ministries, to the head of the administration and the army, a crowd of the best of whom it must be said that no one knows whence he comes, a noisy, disreputable, rapacious bohème that crawls into gallooned coats with the same grotesque dignity as the high dignitaries of Soulouque. One can visualize clearly this upper stratum of the Society of December 10, if one reflects that *Véron-Crevel****** is its preacher of morals and *Granier de Cassagnac* its thinker. When Guizot. at the time of his ministry, utilized this Granier on a

---

* *Etat major*: General Staff.—*Ed.*

** *Vol* means flights and theft. [*Note by Marx.*]

*** "It is the first flight (theft) of the eagle."—*Ed.*

**** "Thou countest thy goods, thou shouldst first count thy years." [*Note by Marx.*]

***** In his work, *Cousine Bette*, Balzac delineates the thoroughly dissolute Parisian philistine in Crevel, a character which he draws after the model of Dr. Véron, the proprietor of the *Constitutionnel*.[56] [*Note by Marx.*]

hole-and-corner newspaper against the dynastic opposition, he used to boast of him with the quip: *"C'est le roi des drôles,"* "he is the king of buffoons." One would do wrong to recall the Regency[57] or Louis XV in connection with Louis Bonaparte's court and clique. For "often already, France has experienced a government of mistresses; but never before a government of *hommes entretenus."**

Driven by the contradictory demands of his situation and being at the same time, like a conjurer, under the necessity of keeping the public gaze fixed on himself, as Napoleon's substitute, by springing constant surprises, that is to say, under the necessity of executing a *coup d'état en miniature* every day, Bonaparte throws the entire bourgeois economy into confusion, violates everything that seemed inviolable to the Revolution of 1848, makes some tolerant of revolution, others desirous of revolution, and produces actual anarchy in the name of order, while at the same time stripping its halo from the entire state machine, profanes it and makes it at once loathsome and ridiculous. The cult of the Holy Tunic of Treves[58] he duplicates at Paris in the cult of the Napoleonic imperial mantle. But when the imperial mantle finally falls on the shoulders of Louis Bonaparte, the bronze statue of Napoleon will crash from the top of the Vendôme Column.

---

* The words quoted are those of Madame Girardin. [*Note by Marx.*]
Hommes entretenus: Kept men.—*Ed.*

MARX TO J. WEYDEMEYER

London, March 5, 1852

Dear Weywy,

I'm afraid things got mixed up a bit because, having misunderstood thy last letter, I addressed the last two packets as follows: "Office of the Revolution, 7, Chamber-street, Box 1817." That confounded "Box 1817" was what caused the mix-up, as you wrote to me to add this appendix to the "old address" without differentiating the first address from the second. But I hope the matter is cleared up before this letter arrives, the more so since last Friday's letter contains the very detailed No. V of my article.* I was prevented from finishing No. VI, the concluding instalment, this week. If your newspaper has appeared again this delay cannot cause any stoppage as you are well provided with material.

Your article against Heinzen, which Engels unfortunately sent me too late, is very good, both coarse and *fine*—a combination which should be found in any polemic worthy of the name. I showed this article to Ernest Jones, and enclosed you will find a communication to you from him intended for publication. As Jones writes very illegibly, with abbreviations, and as I assume that you are not an out-and-out Englishman as yet, I am sending you together with the original a copy made by my wife, and at the same time the German translation, as you must have them both printed side by side, original and translation. To the letter from Jones you can make the following addendum:

---

* K. Marx, *The Eighteenth Brumaire of Louis Bonaparte.* (See present edition pp. 7-135.)—*Ed.*

With regard to *George Julian Harney*, who is also one of Herr Heinzen's authorities, he published our *Communist Manifesto* in English in his *Red Republican*[59] with a marginal note saying that it was "the most revolutionary document ever given to the world," and in his *Democratic Review* he translated the articles I wrote in the *Revue of the Neue Rheinische Zeitung*[60] on the French Revolution,* that work of wisdom "killed" by Heinzen. In an article on Louis Blanc he refers his readers to these articles as the "true criticism" of the French affair. For the rest, in England there is no need to refer only to the "extremists." If a Member of Parliament in England becomes a Minister he has to be re-elected, so *Disraeli,* the new Chancellor of the Exchequer, writes to his constituents on March 1:

"We shall endeavour to terminate that *strife of classes* which of late years has exercised so pernicious an influence over the welfare of this kingdom."

On which *The Times* comments on March 2:

". . . if anything would ever divide classes in this country beyond reconciliation, and leave no chance of a just and honourable peace, it would be a tax on foreign corn."

And in case an ignorant "man of character" like Heinzen should imagine that the aristocracy is *for* and the bourgeoisie *against* corn laws, because the former wants *"monopoly"* and the latter *"freedom"*—a worthy of this sort can tell opposites only in this ideological form—it is to be noted that in the eighteenth century the English aristocracy was for "freedom" (of trade) and the bourgeoisie for "monopoly"—the same relative position that we find at this very moment between these two classes in "Prussia" with regard to "corn laws." The *Neue Preußische Zeitung*[61] is the most violent freetrader.

Finally, in your place I should in general remark to the democratic gentlemen that they would do better first to

---

* The reference is to Marx's *The Class Struggles in France, 1848 to 1850*.

acquaint themselves with bourgeois literature before they presume to yap at the opponents of it. For instance, these gentlemen should study the historical works of Thierry, Guizot, John Wade, and others in order to enlighten themselves as to the past "history of classes." Before they try to criticize the critique of political economy they should acquaint themselves with the fundamentals of political economy. One has only to open Ricardo's great opus, for example, to find these opening words of his Preface on the first page:

"The produce of the earth—all that is derived from its surface by the united application of labour, machinery, and capital—is divided among *three classes* of the community; namely, the proprietor of the land, the owner of the stock or capital necessary for its cultivation, and the labourers by whose industry it is cultivated."*

How far bourgeois society in the United States still is from being mature enough to make the class struggle obvious and comprehensible is most strikingly proved by *C. H. Carey* (of Philadelphia), the only American economist of importance. He attacks *Ricardo*, the most classic representative (interpreter) of the bourgeoisie and the most stoical adversary of the proletariat, as a man whose works are an arsenal for Anarchists, Socialists, and all the enemies of the bourgeois order of society. He reproaches not only him but Malthus, Mill, Say, Torrens, Wakefield, McCulloch, Senior, Whately, R. Jones, and others, the leading economists of Europe, with rending society asunder and preparing civil war because they show that the economic bases of the different classes are bound to give rise to a necessary and ever-growing antagonism among them. He tried to refute them, not indeed like the fatuous Heinzen by connecting the existence of classes with the existence of *political* privileges and *monopolies,* but by attempting to make out that *economic* conditions—

---

* David Ricardo, *Principles of Political Economy and Taxation,* Preface.—*Ed.*

138

rent (landed property), *profit* (capital), and wages (wage labour) instead of being conditions of struggle and antagonism are rather conditions of association and harmony. All he proves, of course, is that he is taking the "undeveloped" conditions of the United States for "normal conditions."

And now as to myself, no credit is due to me for discovering the existence of classes in modern society or the struggle between them. Long before me bourgeois historians had described the historical development of this class struggle and bourgeois economists the economic anatomy of the classes. What I did that was new was to prove: 1) that the *existence of classes* is only bound up with *particular historical phases in the development of production*, 2) that the class struggle necessarily leads to the *dictatorship of the proletariat*, 3) that this dictatorship itself only constitutes the transition to the *abolition of all classes* and to a *classless society*. Ignorant louts like Heinzen, who deny not merely the class struggle but even the existence of classes, only prove that, despite all their blood-curdling yelps and the humanitarian airs they give themselves, they regard the social conditions under which the bourgeoisie rules as the final product, the *non plus ultra** of history, and that they are only the servitors of the bourgeoisie. And the less these louts realize the greatness and transient necessity of the bourgeois regime itself the more disgusting is their servitude.

From the above notes take anything you think suitable. For the rest, Heinzen has adopted "centralization" from us in place of his "federative republic," etc. When the views which we are now spreading about the classes become platitudes and part of the equipment of the "individual with common sense," then that rogue will announce them with a lot of noise as the latest product of "his own penetration" and start barking against our developing the

---

* Highest point attainable.—*Ed.*

point further. So by "his own penetration" he yelped against the Hegelian philosophy as long as it was progressive. Now he is helping himself to the stale crumbs of it which have been spewed out undigested by Ruge.

You are getting herewith the end of the Hungarian correspondence. You must try to pick something from it—if your newspaper exists—the more so since *Szemere*, the former Prime Minister of Hungary, promised me when he was in Paris to write a lengthy article for you *over his own signature.*

If you have managed to get out your paper send *more* copies so that they can be distributed more widely.

Yours,

K. MARX

NOTES

[1] *The Eighteenth Brumaire of Louis Bonaparte* is one of the masterpieces of Marxism. In this important work Marx analysed the events of the Revolution of 1848-51 in France and on the basis of this analysis elaborated further the fundamental tenets of historical materialism, the theory of the class struggle and the proletarian revolution and of the dictatorship of the proletariat. For the first time Marx advanced here the proposition that the victorious proletariat must necessarily smash the bourgeois state machine. The idea of an alliance between the working class and the peasantry was further expounded in this work and Marx drew the conclusion that in bourgeois society irreconcilable contradictions develop between the interests of the peasants and the interests of capital, hence only the urban proletariat can be the natural ally and leader of the peasantry. Marx wrote the book from December 1851 to March 1852, hot on the heels of the events. While working on *The Eighteenth Brumaire of Louis Bonaparte* Marx maintained a constant exchange of opinion with Engels on the French events. In addition to the press and official documents, Marx used also private reports from Paris as source material. At first it was intended to publish *The Eighteenth Brumaire of Louis Bonaparte* as a series of articles in the journal *Die Revolution*, a weekly which J. Weydemeyer—a friend of Marx and Engels and a member of the Communist League—planned to issue in the USA. Weydemeyer, however, succeeded in publishing but two numbers of the journal (in January 1852), before financial difficulties forced him to discontinue publication. Marx's articles arrived too late and were therefore not published in this periodical. At Marx's suggestion Weydemeyer had the work printed as a separate book in May 1852 forming the first (and only) issue of the non-periodical journal *Die Revolution*. He changed the title of the book to *The Eighteenth Brumaire of Louis Napoleon* (instead of Louis Bonaparte). Weydemeyer who was then in straitened circumstances was unable to purchase from the owner of the printing-house the greater part of this first edition and only very few copies reached Europe. Efforts to reprint the book in Germany or England (in an English translation) proved unsuccessful. The second edition of the book came out only in

1869. Marx again went over the text to prepare it for this publication. In his preface to the 1869 edition Marx described the editorial work carried out by him in the following way: "A revision of the present work would have robbed it of its peculiar colouring. Accordingly I have confined myself to mere correction of printer's errors and to striking out allusions now no longer intelligible." The third edition of the book was edited by Engels and was published in 1885 in accordance with the text of the 1869 edition.—7.

2 *Montagne*—in the French Constituent and Legislative Assemblies of 1848-51 a group representing the party of the petty-bourgeois democrats and republicans headed by Ledru-Rollin, who ranged themselves around the newspaper *Réforme*; petty-bourgeois Socialists led by Louis Blanc joined this party.—15.

3 *The Eighteenth Brumaire* (November 9, 1799)—the *coup d'état*, which took place on this day, completed the bourgeois counter-revolutionary development in France and resulted in the establishment of Napoleon Bonaparte's military dictatorship.—15.

4 On December 10, 1848, Louis Bonaparte was elected president of the French Republic by universal ballot.—18.

5 During the exodus of the Israelites from Egypt the hardships of the journey and hunger caused, according to the Bible, the faint-hearted among them longingly to think of the days of captivity when at least they had enough to eat. The phrase *"to long for the fleshpots of Egypt"* has become a proverb.—18.

6 *Hic Rhodus, hic salta!* (Here is Rhodes, leap here!)—these words (from Aesop's fable the *Swaggerer*), addressed to a swaggerer claiming that he had made a remarkable leap in Rhodes, mean "show right here what you can do!"
Here is the rose, here dance!—this paraphrase of the preceding quotation is used by Hegel in the preface to his work *Grundlinien der Philosophie des Rechts* (*Principals of the Philosophy of Right*). In Greek Rhodes, the name of the island, means also "rose."—19.

7 In May 1852 Louis Bonaparte's term of office as president expired. According to the French Constitution of 1848 presidential elections had to take place every four years on the second Sunday in May.—20.

8 *Chiliasm* (from the Greek word *chilias*, a thousand)—a mystical religious doctrine of the second coming of Christ and the establishment of the millennium, when justice, universal equality and

prosperity will be triumphant. Chiliastic beliefs arose in the period of decaying slave society; they were based on the unbearable oppression and suffering of the working people who sought a release in fantastic dreams of deliverance. These beliefs were widespread in early Christian times and later on they were constantly revived in the teachings of various mediaeval sects.—20.

[9] *In partibus infidelium*—in the country of the infidels (added to the title of Catholic bishops appointed to a purely nominal diocese in non-Christian countries), that is non-existent in reality.—20.

[10] "...Den alles, was entsteht, ist wert, daß es zu Grunde geht." Goethe, *Faust*, Erster Teil, Studierzimmer, Zeilen 1339-40 (Goethe, *Faust*, Part One, Lines 1339-40)—21.

[11] In the German edition of 1869 and also in those of 1852 and 1885 the date for the opening of the Legislative Assembly is given erroneously as May 29, 1849.—21.

[12] *Dynastic opposition*—a group, led by Odilon Barrot, in the French Chamber of Deputies during the July Monarchy. The representatives of this group, voicing the sentiments of the liberal circles of the industrial and commercial bourgeoisie, advocated a moderate electoral reform as a means of averting the revolution and preserving the Orleans dynasty.—21.

[13] *Crapulinski*—the hero of Heine's poem, *Zwei Ritter* (*Two Knights*), a spendthrift Polish nobleman; the name Crapulinski comes from the French word *crapule*—intemperance, gluttony, drunkenness, and also—loafer, scoundrel.
Here Marx alludes to Louis Bonaparte.—26.

[14] *Le National*—a French daily, published in Paris from 1830 to 1851; the organ of the moderate bourgeois republicans.—27.

[15] *Journal des Débats*—abbreviated form of the French bourgeois daily *Journal des Débats politiques et littéraires,* founded in Paris in 1789. During the July Monarchy—a government paper, the organ of the pro-Orleans bourgeoisie. During the Revolution of 1848 the newspaper expressed the views of the counter-revolutionary bourgeoisie, the so-called party of Order.—27.

[16] *The Constitutional Charter* adopted after the bourgeois Revolution of 1830 in France, was the basic law of the July Monarchy. Nominally the Charter proclaimed the sovereign rights of the nation and somewhat restricted the king's power. At the same time, however, it

left untouched the police and bureaucratic machinery and the severe laws against the labour and democratic movement.—29.

[17] *"Frère, il faut mourir!"* ["Brother, death is near!"]—with these words members of the Roman Catholic monastic Order of Trappists greet each other. The Trappist Order, which originated in 1664, is distinguished by the strictness of its rules and the ascetic life led by its members.—32.

[18] *Clichy*—from 1826 to 1867 a debtor's prison in Paris.—32.

[19] *Praetorians*—in ancient Rome the life-guards of the general or emperor, maintained by him and enjoying various privileges.—35.

[20] From May to July 1849 the Kingdom of Naples took part in the intervention against the Republic of Rome.
The Constituent Assembly of Rome, elected on the basis of universal suffrage, abolished the secular power of the Pope and proclaimed the republic on February 9, 1849. The executive power of the Roman Republic was concentrated in the hands of a triumvirate headed by Mazzini. While the Republic was in existence a number of bourgeois-democratic reforms were carried out. However, the limited class character of the Republic affected its agrarian policy—the refusal to hand over the landlords' estates to the peasants as their property deprived the Republic of valuable allies in its fight against the counter-revolution. The intervention of France, Austria and Naples led to the fall of the Republic on July 3, 1849.—35.

[21] Marx alludes to the following events in Louis Bonaparte's life: in 1832 Louis Bonaparte became a Swiss citizen in the canton Thurgau; in 1848 during his stay in Britain he voluntarily joined the special constabulary who together with the police took part in actions against the workers' demonstration, organized by the Chartists on April 10, 1848.—35.

[22] This refers to the analysis of the election of December 10, 1848 given by Marx in his work *Die Klassenkämpfe in Frankreich 1848 bis 1850* (*The Class Struggles in France, 1848 to 1850*). (See K. Marx and F. Engels, *Selected Works,* Vol. I, Moscow 1958, pp. 173-75.)—36.

[23] *Legitimists*—supporters of the "legitimate" Bourbon dynasty that ruled France till 1792, and also during the Restoration (1814-30).
Orleanists—supporters of the House of Orleans that came to power during the July Revolution of 1830 and was overthrown by the Revolution of 1848.—36.

[24] *Party of Order*—a coalition of the two French monarchist factions, the Legitimists and Orleanists. This party of the conservative big bourgeoisie came into being in 1848; from 1849 till the *coup d'état* of December 2, 1851 it held the leading position in the Legislative Assembly of the Second Republic. The moral bankruptcy of its policy directed against the people was utilized by the Louis Bonaparte clique for its own Bonapartist aims.—36.

[25] Caligula, the Roman emperor (A. D. 37-41) was enthroned by the Praetorian guard.—39.

[26] The French Government obtained an appropriation from the Constituent Assembly for the dispatch of an expeditionary corps to Italy in April 1849, on the pretext of giving support to Piedmont in its fight against Austria and protecting the Roman Republic. However, the true purpose of the expedition was intervention against the Republic of Rome and restoration of the Pope's secular power.—40.

[27] *Moniteur*—short for *Le Moniteur universel*, French daily, official organ of the government; under this name it was published in Paris from 1789 to 1869.—40.

[28] This refers to the bill tabled on November 6, 1851, by the royalists Le Flô, Baze and Panat, the quaestors of the Legislative Assembly (charged by the Assembly with handling economic and financial matters and safeguarding its security) which was, after a heated debate, rejected on November 17. During the ballot the *Montagne* supported the Bonapartists, as it saw in the royalists the main danger.—40.

[29] *Peter Schlemihl*—the hero of Chamisso's fairy-tale *Peter Schlemihl*, who exchanged his shadow for a magic purse.—44.

[30] *Ems*—spa in Germany. In August 1849 a Legitimist conference was held here; it was attended by the Count of Chambord, the pretender to the French throne under the name of Henry V.
Claremont—a castle near London, Louis Philippe's residence after his escape from France.—48.

[31] Article V belongs to the introductory part of the French Constitution of 1848; for articles in the main body of the Constitution Arabic numerals are used.—51.

[32] An allusion to Louis Bonaparte's plans, who expected that Pope Pius IX would place the French crown on his head. According to biblical tradition David, the King of Israel, was anointed king by the prophet Samuel.—57.

[33] An allusion to Louis Bonaparte's Book *Des idées napoléoniennes*, published in Paris in 1839. (*Napoléon*-Louis Bonaparte, *Des idées napoléoniennes*, Paris, 1839.)—63.

[34] *Burgrave*s was the name given to the 17 leading Orleanists and Legitimists, who were members of the Legislative Assembly's committee for draughting a new electoral law, for their unwarranted claim to power and their reactionary aspirations. The name has been taken from the title of Victor Hugo's historical drama. Its action is set in mediaeval Germany where a Burg-Graf was the ruler of a "Burg"—a fortified town or castle—appointed by the emperor.—69.

[35] The press law passed by the Legislative Assembly in July 1850 considerably increased the deposits which the publishers of newspapers had to pay, and introduced a stamp duty which applied to pamphlets as well. The new law continued the reactionary measures which meant that in practice freedom of the press was abolished in France.—70.

[36] *La Presse*—a bourgeois daily, published in Paris since 1836; in 1848 and 1849 it was the organ of the bourgeois republicans, afterwards a Bonapartist paper.—70.

[37] This passage refers to the efforts Louis Bonaparte made during the July Monarchy to carry out a *coup d'état* by means of a military insurrection. On September 30, 1836, he succeeded in rousing two artillery regiments of the Strasbourg garrison with the aid of a few pro-Bonapartist officers, but within a few hours the insurgents were disarmed. Louis Bonaparte was arrested and deported to America. Taking advantage of a certain revival of Bonapartist feelings in France, he landed with a handful of conspirators in Boulogne on August 6, 1840, and attempted to instigate a rebellion among the troops of the local garrison. But this attempt too proved to be an utter failure. Bonaparte was sentenced to life imprisonment, but in 1846 he escaped to England.—76.

[38] *Schufterle* and *Spiegelberg*—characters in Schiller's drama *Die Räuber (The Robbers)*, who plunder and murder unimpeded by any moral scruples.—77.

[39] *Elysée newspapers*—those of a Bonapartist trend; the name is taken from the Elysée palace, the Paris residence of Louis Bonaparte while president.—79.

[40] For his play on words Marx utilizes here a line from Schiller's *Lied an die Freude (Ode to Joy)*, in which the poet sings of joy as

the "daughter of Elysium." In classical mythology Elysium or Elysian fields is equivalent to paradise. Champs Elysée (Elysian Fields) was the name of the Paris avenue, where Louis Bonaparte's residence stood.—84.

[41] *Parliaments*—in France before the Bourgeois Revolution of 1789 parliaments were high judicial bodies. They existed in a number of towns throughout the country. The most important was the Paris Parliament, which registered the royal decrees and possessed the right of remonstrance as it was called, i.e., the right to protest against decrees which infringed the customs and the legislation of the country. However, the parliamentary opposition was in fact powerless, since the personal appearance of the king at the session made registration of the decrees obligatory.—89.

[42] *Belle Isle*—an island in the Bay of Biscay; from 1849 to 1857 it served as a place of detention for political prisoners; in particular the workers who took part in the Paris uprising of June 1848 were imprisoned there.—93.

[43] Marx paraphrases here a story which the Greek writer Athenaeus recounts (2nd-3rd century A. D.) in his book *Deipnosophistae (Dinner-Table Philosophers)*. The Egyptian Pharaoh Tachos alluding to the small stature of the Spartan King Agesilaus who had come with his troops to the Pharaoh's assistance, said: "The mountain was in labour. Zeus was scared. But the mountain has brought forth a mouse." Agesilaus replied: "I seem to thee a mouse, but the time will come when I will appear to thee as a lion."—94.

[44] *Assemblée Nationale*—a monarchist daily published in Paris from 1848 to 1857.—98.

[45] In the fifties of the 19th century the Count of Chambord, the Legitimist pretender to the French throne lived in Venice.—98.

[46] This refers to tactical disagreements in the Legitimist camp during the Restoration period. Louis XVIII and Villèle favoured a more cautious introduction of reactionary measures, while the Count d'Artois (from 1824 King Charles X) and Polignac completely ignored conditions in France and advocated the unqualified restoration of the pre-revolutionary regime.

During the Restoration period the *Palace of the Tuileries* was Louis XVIII's residence; the Count d'Artois lived in the *Pavillon Marsan,* one of the Palace's wings.—100.

[47] The first international trade and industrial exhibition was held in London from May to October 1851.—108.

[48] *The Economist,* January 10, 1852, pp. 29-30.—110.

[49] *Le Messager de l'Assemblée*—French anti-Bonapartist daily; published in Paris from February 16 to December 2, 1851.—111.

[50] A paraphrase from Shakespeare's *Hamlet,* Act I, Scene 5.—121.

[51] *Code Napoléon*—a civil code, published by Napoleon in 1804, it was also introduced in the parts of West and South-West Germany that were conquered by the French, in the Rhine Province it remained in force after the latter had been incorporated in Prussia. Engels called it the "classic law code of bourgeois society."—124.

[52] *Cevennes*—a mountainous region in the Languedoc, South-East France where from 1702 to 1705 an uprising of peasants (the so-called Camisards) took place. The revolt, which began as a protest against the persecution of Protestants, became strongly anti-feudal in character. Separate outbreaks of the uprising continued to occur till 1715.

Vendée—Western Department of France, during the French Bourgeois Revolution of the end of the eighteenth century the scene of a counter-revolutionary peasant revolt, led by the nobility and clergy.—125.

[53] In place of the last two sentences of this paragraph the following lines were printed in the 1852 edition: "The demolition of the state machine will not endanger centralization. Bureaucracy is only the low and brutal form of a centralization that is still afflicted with its opposite, with feudalism. When he is disappointed in the Napoleonic Restoration, the French peasant will part with his belief in his small holding, the entire state edifice erected on this small holding will fall to the ground and *the proletarian revolution will obtain that chorus without which its solo song becomes the swan song in all peasant countries.*"—131.

[54] *The Council of Constance* (1414-18) was convened for the purpose of strengthening the position of the Roman Catholic Church which had been weakened by the rising Reformation movement. The Council condemned the teachings of John Wycliffe and Jan Hus, the leaders of the Reformation. It healed the schism in the Catholic Church by electing a new Pope in place of the three pretenders who had been contending with each other for the papal tiara.—131.

[55] A reference to the German or "True" Socialism—a reactionary trend which became widespread chiefly among petty-bourgeois intellectuals in Germany during the forties of the last century. The representatives of "True Socialism"—Karl Grün, Moses Hess, Hermann Kriege, etc.—replaced socialist ideas by sentimental sermons on love and

brotherhood and denied the necessity of a bourgeois-democratic revolution in Germany. Marx's and Engels's criticism of this trend can be found in the following of their works: *Deutsche Ideologie* (*The German Ideology*), "*Der Volkstribun*" [*The People's Tribune*], Edited by *Hermann Kriege, Deutscher Sozialismus in Versen und Prosa* (*German Socialism in Verse and Prose*), *Das Manifest der Kommunistischen Partei* (*Manifesto of the Communist Party*).—132.

[56] *Le Constitutionnel*—a French bourgeois daily, published in Paris from 1815 to 1870; in the forties it was the newspaper of the moderate wing of the Orleanists; during the Revolution of 1848 it expressed the views of the counter-revolutionary bourgeoisie centred around Thiers; after the *coup d'état* of December 1851 it became a Bonapartist paper.—134.

[57] A reference to Philippe d'Orleans's regency during the infancy of Louis XV from 1715 to 1723.—135.

[58] *The Holy Tunic of Treves*—a Catholic relic preserved in the Treves Cathedral, alleged to be a holy vestment taken from Christ while he was suffering death. It was regarded by pilgrims as an object of veneration.—135.

[59] *The Red Republican*—a Chartist weekly published by G. J. Harney from July to November 1850. The first English translation of the *Communist Manifesto* was published in this weekly.—137.

[60] *Neue Rheinische Zeitung. Politisch-ökonomische Revue* (*New Rhenish Gazette. Political and Economic Review*)—a journal founded by Marx and Engels in December 1849 and issued by them till November 1850. The journal was the theoretical and political organ of the Communist League and a continuation of *Neue Rheinische Zeitung* published by Marx and Engels during the Revolution of 1848-49. In all six numbers of the journal came out from March to November 1850, including one double issue (5-6). It was edited in London and printed in Hamburg. New York was also mentioned on the cover, for Marx and Engels expected that the journal would also be distributed among the German emigrants in America. The by far greater part of the material printed (articles, surveys, reviews) was written by Marx and Engels, who also encouraged their supporters—Wilhelm Wolff, Joseph Weydemeyer, J. G. Eccarius—to send contributions. Among the works of the founders of Marxism published in the journal are *Die Klassenkämpfe in Frankreich 1848 bis 1850* (*The Class Struggles in France, 1848 to 1850*) by Marx and *Die deutsche Reichsverfassungskampagne* (*Campaign for a Constitution of the German Empire*) and *Der deutsche Bauernkrieg* (*The Peasant War in Germany*) by Engels. The papers

published in the journal summed up the results of the Revolution of 1848-49 and further elaborated the theory and the tactics of the revolutionary proletarian party. The periodical ceased publication because of the political oppression in Germany and lack of funds.—137

⁶¹ *Neue Preussische Zeitung (New Prussian Gazette)*—a German daily which began to appear in Berlin in June 1848; it was the organ of the counter-revolutionary camarilla at the Prussian court and of the Prussian Junkers. The paper was also known as *Kreuz-Zeitung (Cross Gazette)*, because of the cross in its heading.—137.

BIOGRAPHICAL INDEX

A

Aesop (6th cent. B. C.)—semi-legendary Greek fabulist.—19.

Agesilaus II (c. 442—c. 358 B. C.)—King of Sparta (c 399-c. 358 B. C.)—94.

Ailly, Pierre d' (1350-1420 or 1425)—French cardinal, well-known theologian; played an important part at the Council of Constance.—131.

Alexander of Macedon (356-323 B. C.).—78.

Alais, Louis Pierre Constant (born c. 1821)—French police agent.—77, 82.

Anglès, François Ernest (1807-1861)—French landowner, deputy to the Legislative Assembly (1850-51), representing the party of Order.—104.

B

Bailly, Jean Sylvain (1736-1793) —French astronomer, took an active part in the French Bourgeois Revolution of the end of the 18th century, one of the leaders of the liberal constitutionalist bourgeoisie.—17.

Balzac, Honoré de (1799-1850). —134.

Baraguay d'Hilliers, Achille (1795-1878)—French general, since 1854 marshal; during the Second Republic deputy to the Constituent and Legislative Assemblies, in 1851 commander of the Paris garrison; Bonapartist.—87, 88, 102.

Baroche, Pierre Jules (1802-1870)—French politician, lawyer, during the Second Republic deputy to the Constituent and Legislative Assemblies, represented the party of Order; in 1849 General Procurator of the Court of Appeal; Bonapartist, member of several Cabinets before and after the *coup d'état* of December 2, 1851—69, 82, 88, 94.

Barrot, Odilon (1791-1873)— French bourgeois politician, up to February 1848 leader of the liberal monarchist opposition; from December 1848 to October 1849 headed the government, which relied on the support of the counter-revolutionary monarchist bloc.—37, 38, 40, 44, 60, 61, 63, 73, 90, 93, 100, 111.

Baze, Jean Didier (1800-1881)—French lawyer and politician, during the Second Republic deputy to the Constituent and Legislative Assemblies; Orleanist.—99, 116.

Bedeau, Marie Alphonse (1804-1863)—French general and politician, moderate bourgeois republican; during the Second Republic Vice-President of the Constituent and Legislative Assemblies.—43, 89.

Benoit d'Azy, Denis (1796-1880)—French politician, financier and industrialist; Vice-President of the Legislative Assembly (1849-51), Legitimist.—93, 99.

Bernard—French colonel, who headed the military commissions which inflicted punishment on the participants of the Paris uprising of June 1848; after the *coup d'état* of December 2, 1851 was one of the organizers of judicial prosecutions against the anti-Bonapartist republicans.—34.

Berryer, Pierre Antoine (1790-1868)—French lawyer and politician, during the Second Republic deputy to the Constituent and Legislative Assemblies, Legitimist.—49, 68, 90, 99, 100, 107.

Billault, Auguste Adolphe Marie (1805-1863)—French politician, lawyer, Orleanist, member of the Constituent Assem-

bly (1848-49); after 1849 Bonapartist, Minister of Interior (1854-58).—93.

Blanc, Louis (1811-1882)—French petty-bourgeois Socialist, historian; in 1848 member of the Provisional Government and Chairman of the Luxembourg Commission—"a government commission on the labour question," which acted as a mediator between workers and employers; took up a conciliatory attitude towards the bourgeoisie; in August 1848 emigrated to England and was a leader of the petty-bourgeois émigrés in London.—15, 137.

Blanqui, Louis Auguste (1805-1881)—French revolutionary, utopian Communist, advocated conspiratorial methods and was the leader of the secret society, *Société des saisons,* and organizer of the revolt of May 12, 1839; during the Revolution of 1848 stood on the extreme Left wing of the democratic and proletarian movement in France; was many times sentenced to terms of imprisonment.—22.

Bonaparte, Louis—See *Napoleon III.*

Bourbon—royal dynasty which reigned in France from 1589 to 1792, 1814-15 and 1815-30.—36, 46, 47, 95, 97, 99, 123.

Broglie, Achille Charles Léonce Victor, duke (1785-1870)—French statesman, Prime Minister (1835-36), deputy to the Legislative Assembly (1849-51), Orleanist.—68, 100.

Brutus, Marcus Junius (c. 85-42 B. C.)—Roman politician, one of the leaders of the aristocratic republican conspiracy against Julius Caesar.—16.

C

Caesar, Gaius Julius (c. 100-44 B. C.)—16.

Caligula, Gaius Caesar (12-41 A. D.)—Roman emperor (37-41)—38.

Carey, Henry Charles (1793-1879)—American bourgeois economist, propounded the theory of class harmony.—138.

Carlier, Pierre (1799-1858)—Prefect of the Paris police (1849-51), Bonapartist.—63, 77, 84, 112.

Caussidière, Marc (1808-1861)—French petty-bourgeois democrat, participated in the Lyons insurrection of 1834; during the July Monarchy an organizer of secret revolutionary societies; after the February Revolution of 1848 Prefect of the Paris police, deputy to the Constituent Assembly; in June 1848 emigrated to England.—15.

Cavaignac, Louis Eugène (1802-1857)—French general and politician, moderate bourgeois republican; took part in the conquest of Algeria, after the February Revolution of 1848 governor of Algeria, during the war he distinguished himself by the use of barbarous methods; since May 1848 French War Minister, he put down the June uprising of the Paris proletariat with the utmost cruelty; head of the executive power from June to December 1848.—28, 34, 35, 36, 45, 91, 105, 116.

Chambord, Henri Charles, Count (1820-1883)—the last representative of the older branch of the Bourbon dynasty, grandson of Charles X, pretender to the French throne under the name of Henry V.—98.

Chamisso, Adelbert von (1781-1838)—German romantic poet, came out against feudal reaction.—43.

Changarnier, Nicolas Anne Théodule (1793-1877)—French general and bourgeois politician, monarchist; during the Second Republic deputy to the Constituent and Legislative Assemblies; after June 1848 commander of the Paris garrison and the National Guard, took part in dispersing the Paris demonstration of June 13, 1849.—39, 41, 44, 52, 57, 58, 77-79, 82, 86-91, 94, 101, 104, 111, 114, 116.

Charras, Jean Baptiste Adolphe (1810-1865)—French soldier and politician, moderate bourgeois republican; took part in quelling the uprising of Paris workers in June 1848; during the Second Republic deputy to the Constituent and Legislative Assemblies, opponent of Louis Bonaparte; after the *coup d'état* of December 2, 1851 he was deported.—8, 116.

Constant, Benjamin (1767-1830)—French liberal bourgeois

Fould, Achille (1800-1867) — French banker and politician, Orleanist, later Bonapartist, between 1849 and 1867 he was several times Minister of Finance.—63, 88, 94, 103.

G

Girardin, Delphine, de (1804-1855) —French writer, wife of Émile de Girardin.—135.

Girardin, Émile de (1806-1881) —French bourgeois publicist and politician, from 1830's to 1860's edited, with several interruptions, the newspaper *La Presse,* in politics distinguished himself by his complete lack of principles; before the Revolution of 1848 he opposed the Guizot government, during the Revolution— a bourgeois republican, deputy to the Legislative Assembly (1850-51); subsequently a Bonapartist.—85.

Giraud, Charles Joseph Barthélémy (1802-1881) —French lawyer, monarchist, Minister of Education (1851).—112.

Gracchus, Gaius Sempronius (153-121 B. C.) —Roman tribune (123-122 B. C.), fought for the introduction of agrarian laws in the interests of the peasantry; brother of Tiberius Gracchus.—16.

Gracchus, Tiberius Sempronius (163-133 B. C.) —Roman tribune (133 B. C.), fought for the introduction of agrarian laws in the interests of the peasants.—16.

Granier de Cassagnac, Adolphe (1806-1880) —French journalist, unscrupulous politician, before the Revolution of 1848 Orleanist, later Bonapartist; during the Second Empire member of the Legislative Corps.—134.

Guize, Henri II de Lorraine, duke (1614-1664) —took part in the Fronde—a social movement against absolutism in France from 1648 to 1653.— 133.

Guizot, François Pierre Guillaume (1787-1874) —French bourgeois historian and statesman, from 1840 up to the February Revolution of 1848 he in fact directed the domestic and foreign policy, voicing the interests of the big finance bourgeoisie.—16, 31, 99, 100, 120, 134, 138.

H

Harney, George Julian (1817-1897) —outstanding figure in the English labour movement, one of the Left-wing leaders of the Chartist movement; editor of the *Northern Star,* friend of Marx and Engels.— 137.

Hautpoul, Alphonse Henri d' (1789-1865) —French general, Legitimist, later Bonapartist; deputy to the Legislative Assembly (1849-51), War Minister (1849-50).—63, 69, 78-80.

Hegel, Georg Wilhelm Friedrich (1770-1831) —outstanding representative of German classic philosophy, he propounded an objective idealism and has most comprehensively elaborated idealist dialectics.—15.

Heine, Heinrich (1797-1856)—25.

Heinzen, Karl (1809-1880)—German radical publicist, petty-bourgeois democrat, an opponent of Marx and Engels; in 1849 he participated in the uprising in Baden and the Palatinate, then he emigrated to Switzerland and subsequently to England; in the autumn of 1850 he finally settled in the U.S.A.—136, 137, 138, 139.

Henry V—see Chambord, Henri Charles.

Henry VI (1421-1471)—King of England (1422-1461).—97.

Hugo, Victor Marie (1802-1885). —7, 61.

J

Joinville, de, François Ferdinand Philippe Louis Marie d'Orléans, prince (1818-1900)—son of Louis Philippe, emigrated to England after the Revolution of 1848.—99, 100, 111.

Jones, Ernest Charles (1819-1869)—outstanding figure of the English labour movement, proletarian poet and publicist, a leader of the Left wing of Chartism, one of the editors of the *Northern Star,* editor of the *Notes to the People* and *People's Paper;* friend of Marx and Engels.—136.

Jones, Richard (1790-1855)—English economist.—138.

L

La Hitte, Jean Ernest (1789-1878)—French general, Bonapartist, deputy to the Legislative Assembly (1850-51), Foreign Minister (1849-51).—68.

Lamartine, Alphonse (1790-1869)—French poet, historian and politician, in the 1840's bourgeois republican; in 1848 Foreign Minister and actual head of the Provisional Government.—93.

Lamoricière, Louis Christophe Léon (1806-1865)—French general and politician, moderate bourgeois republican, in 1848 he took an active part in crushing the June uprising, later War Minister in the Cavaignac government (June to December 1848), during the Second Republic deputy to the Constituent and Legislative Assemblies.—45, 116.

La Rochejaquelein, Henri Auguste Georges, marquis (1805-1867)—French politician, member of the Chamber of Peers, one of the leaders of the Legitimist party, during the Second Republic deputy to the Constituent and Legislative Assemblies; later Senator in the Second Empire.—100.

Ledru-Rollin, Alexandre Auguste (1807-1874)—French publicist and politician, one of the leaders of the petty-bourgeois democrats, editor of the newspaper *Réforme;* in 1848 member of the Provisional Government, deputy to the Constituent and Legislative Assemblies, where he led the *Montagne,* after the demonstration of June 13, 1849 emigrated to England.—28, 45, 52, 55.

Le Flô, Adolphe Emmanuel Charles (1804-1887)—French general, politician and diplomat; representative of the party of Order, during the Second Republic deputy to the Constituent and Legislative Assemblies; War Minister in the "Government of National Defence" (1870-71).—40, 116.

Locke, John (1632-1704).—17.

Louis XIV (1638-1715)—King of France (1643-1715).—125.

Louis XV (1710-1774)—King of France (1715-74).—135.

Louis XVIII (1755-1824)—King of France (1814-15 and 1815-24).—16.

Louis Philippe (1773-1850)—Duke of Orleans, King of France (1830-48).—21, 23, 27, 28, 29, 35, 37, 44, 58, 60, 74, 98, 99, 102, 103, 122.

Louis Philippe Albert, Duke of Orleans, Count of Paris (1838-1894)—grandson of King Louis Philippe, pretender to the French throne.—99.

Luther, Martin (1483-1546)—outstanding figure of the Reformation, founder of the Protestant (Lutheran) Church in Germany; ideologist of the German middle class; in 1525 during the Peasant War he sided with the princes and publicly denounced the insurgent peasants and urban poor.—15.

M

McCulloch, John Ramsay (1789-1864)—English bourgeois economist, representative of vulgar political economy.—138.

Magnan, Bernard Pierre (1791-1865)—French general, since December 1851 marshal, Bonapartist; took part in suppressing the workers' insurrections in Lyons (1831 and 1849), Lille and Roubaix (1845) and the Paris uprising of June 1848; deputy to the Legislative Assembly (1849-51), one of the organizers of the *coup d'état* of December 2, 1851.—102, 112, 115.

Maleville, Léon (1803-1879)—French politician, Orleanist, during the Second Republic deputy to the Constituent and Legislative Assemblies, Minister of Interior (second half of December 1848).—93.

Malthus, Thomas Robert (1766-1834)—English clergyman, bourgeois economist, ideologist of the land aristocracy that has become bourgeois, put forward a reactionary theory of population.—138.

Marrast, Armand (1801-1852)—French publicist and politician, a leader of the moderate bourgeois republicans, editor of the newspaper *Le National;* in 1843 member of the Provisional Government and mayor of Paris, President of the Constituent Assembly (1848-49).—17, 29, 40, 41.

Marx, Karl (1818-1883).—7, 13, 14, 136.

Masaniello (original name Tommaso Aniello) (1620-1647) — fisherman, leader of the popular uprising at Naples in 1647 against Spanish dominion— 114.

Mauguin, François (1785-1854) —French lawyer and politician, up to 1848 one of the leaders of the liberal monarchist opposition; during the Second Republic deputy to the Constituent and Legislative Assemblies, sided with the Right-wing deputies.—81, 82, 83.

Maupas, Charlemagne Emile (1818-1888)—French lawyer, Bonapartist, Prefect of the Paris police (1851), one of the organizers of the *coup d'état* of December 2, 1851, Police Minister (1852-53).—112.

Mill, James (1773-1836) — English philosopher, historian and economist.—138.

Molé, Louis Mathieu, count (1781-1855)—French statesman, Orleanist, Prime Minister (1836-37, 1837-39), during the Second Republic deputy to the Constituent and Legislative Assemblies.—68, 100.

Monk, George (1608-1670) — English general, took an active part in the English Bourgeois Revolution of the 17th century; in 1660 he helped to restore the monarchy in England.—78.

Montalembert, Charles (1810-1870)—French politician and writer, during the Second Republic deputy to the Constituent and Legislative Assemblies, Orleanist, leader of Catholic circles; supported Louis Bonaparte during the *coup d'état* of December 2, 1851.—90, 100, 130.

Morny, Charles Auguste Louis Joseph, count (1811-1865) — French politician, Bonapartist, deputy to the Legislative Assembly (1849-51), one of the organizers of the *coup d'état* of December 2, 1851, Minister of Interior (December 1851-January 1852).—134.

N

Napoleon I (Bonaparte) (1769-1821)—Emperor of the French (1804-14 and 1815).—7, 16, 17, 18, 76, 115, 119, 122, 124, 125, 126, 127, 128, 135.

Napoleon III (Louis Napoleon Bonaparte) (1808-1873) — nephew of Napoleon I, President of the Second Republic (1848-51), Emperor of the French (1852-70).—7, 8, 18, 25, 27, 35, 37, 38, 39, 40, 44, 45, 49, 50, 52, 56-59, 60, 61, 63, 67-70, 73-81, 83-94, 95, 96, 100-103, 105-107, 110-117, 120, 122-127, 128-138, 135.

Neumayer, Maximilien Georges Joseph (1789-1866)—French general, sided with the party of Order, commander of the Paris troops (1848-50).—78.

Ney, Edgar (1812-1882) — French officer, Bonapartist, adjutant of President Louis Bonaparte, deputy to the Legislative Assembly (1850-51). —61.

O

Orleans—French royal dynasty (1830-1848).—36, 46, 47, 60, 98, 99, 123, 133, 134.

Orleans, Hélène, née Mecklenburg-Schwerin, duchess (1814-1858)—widow of Ferdinand, King Louis Philippe's elder son, mother of the Count of Paris, the pretender to the French throne.—28, 61.

Oudinot, Nicolas Charles Victor (1791-1863)—French general, Orleanist, during the Second Republic deputy to the Constituent and Legislative Assemblies; in 1849 he commanded the troops dispatched against the Republic of Rome, tried to organize resistance to the *coup d'état* of December 2, 1851.—40, 56, 61.

P

Paris, count—see Louis Philippe Albert, Duke of Orleans.

Perrot, Benjamin Pierre (1791-1865)—French general, took part in quelling the Paris uprising of June 1848, in 1849 commander of the Paris National Guard.—88.

Persigny, Jean Gilbert Victor, count (1808-1872)—French statesman, Bonapartist, deputy to the Legislative Assembly (1849-51), one of the organizers of the *coup d'état* of December 2, 1851, Minister of Interior (1852-54 and 1860-63). —94, 111.

Polignac, Auguste Jules Armand Marie, prince (1780-1847)— French statesman of the Restoration period, Legitimist and Clerical, Foreign Minister and head of the Cabinet (1829-30).—100.

Proudhon, Pierre Joseph (1809-1865)—French writer, economist and sociologist, ideologist of the petty bourgeoisie, one of the originators of anarchism, in 1848 member of the Constituent Assembly.—7, 55.

Publicola, Publius Valerius (d. 503 B.C.)—semi-legendary Roman statesman.—16.

R

Rateau, Jean Pierre (1800-1887) —French lawyer, during the Second Republic deputy to the Constituent and Legislative Assemblies, Bonapartist. —38.

Regnault de Saint-Jean d'Angély, Auguste Michel Etienne, count (1794-1870)—French general, Bonapartist, during the Second Republic deputy to the Constituent and Legislative Assemblies, War Minister (January 1851).—87, 88.

Rémusat, Charles François Marie, count (1797-1875)—French statesman and writer, Orleanist, Minister of Interior (1840), during the Second Republic deputy to the Constituent and Legislative Assemblies, Foreign Minister (1871-73).—89.

Ricardo, David (1772-1823).— 138.

Richard III (1452-1485)—King of England (1483-85).—97.

Robespierre, Maximilien (1758-1794)—outstanding figure of the French Bourgeois Revolution of the end of the 18th century, leader of the Jacobins, head of the revolutionary government (1793-94).—15, 16.

Rouher, Eugène (1814-1884)—French statesman, Bonapartist, during the Second Republic deputy to the Constituent and Legislative Assemblies, Minister of Justice (1849-52, with interruptions); occupied various government posts in the Second Empire.—81, 94.

Royer-Collard, Pierre Paul (1763-1845)—French philosopher and politician, supporter of constitutional monarchy. —16.

Ruge, Arnold (1802-1880)—German publicist, young Hegelian; bourgeois radical, in 1848 deputy to the Frankfort National Assembly, belonging to its Left wing; in the fifties one of the leaders of the German petty-bourgeois emigration in England; after 1866 National Liberal.—140.

S

Saint-Arnaud, Armand Jacques Leroy de (1801-1854)—French general, since 1852 marshal, Bonapartist; War Minister (1851-54), one of the organizers of the *coup d'état* of December 2, 1851, in 1854 Commander-in-Chief of the French army in the Crimea.—40.

Sainte-Beuve, Pierre Henri (1819-1855)—French manufacturer and landowner, supporter of free-trade policy, representative of the party of Order; in the Second Republic member of the Constituent and Legislative Assemblies.—104.

Saint-Jean d'Angely—see Regnault de Saint-Jean d'Angely.

Saint-Just, Louis Antoine (1767-1794)—outstanding figure in the French Bourgeois Revolution of the end of the 18th century, one of the Jacobin leaders.—16.

Saint-Priest, Emmanuel Louis Marie, viscount (1789-1881)—French general and diplomat, Legitimist, deputy to the Legislative Assembly (1849-51). —99.

Sallandrouze, Charles Jean (1808-1867)—French industrialist, deputy to the Constituent Assembly (1848-49); supported Louis Bonaparte during the *coup d'état* of December 2, 1851.—115.

Salvandy, Narcisse Achille, count (1795-1856)—French writer and statesman, Orleanist, Minister of Education (1837-39 and 1845-48).—98.

Say, Jean Baptiste (1767-1832)—French bourgeois economist, a representative of vulgar political economy.—15, 138.

Schiller, Friedrich von (1759-1805).—77, 84.

Schramm, Jean Paul Adam de (1789-1884)—French general and politician, Bonapartist, War Minister (1850-51).—79.

Senior, Nassau William (1790-1864)—English bourgeois vulgar economist.—138.

Shakespeare, William (1564-1616).—121.

Sismondi, Jean Charles Léonard Simonde de (1773-1842)— Swiss economist, criticized capitalism from petty-bourgeois positions.—9.

Soulouque, Faustin (c. 1782-1867)—President of the Negro Republic of Haiti, in 1849 he proclaimed himself emperor, assuming the name of Faustin I.—134.

Sue, Eugène (1804-1857)— French writer, author of novels on social themes, deputy to the Legislative Assembly (1850-51).—70.

Szemere, Barthelemy (1812-1869)—Hungarian politician and publicist; in 1849 Prime Minister of the Hungarian Revolutionary Government; after the defeat of the Hungarian Revolution he emigrated —140.

T

Thierry, Augustin (1795-1856)— French liberal historian.—138.

Thiers, Louis Adolphe (1797-1877)—French bourgeois historian and statesman, Prime Minister (1836, 1840); in the Second Republic deputy to the Constituent and Legislative Assemblies, Orleanist; President of the Republic (1871-73), hangman of the Paris Commune.—40, 49, 52, 56, 68, 90, 99, 100, 101, 104, 107, 111, 114, 116.

Thorigny, Pierre Francois Elisabeth (1798-1869)—French lawyer, Bonapartist, Minister of Interior (1851).—112.

Tocqueville, Alexis (1805-1859) —French bourgeois historian and politician, Legitimist and advocate of constitutional monarchy, in the Second Republic deputy to the Constituent and Legislative Assemblies, Foreign Minister (June-October 1849).—101.

V

Vaïsse, Claude Marius (1799-1864)—French statesman, Bonapartist; Minister of Interior (January-April 1851).—92.

Vatimesnil, Antoine François Henri (1789-1860)—French politician, Legitimist, Minister of Education (1828-30), deputy to the Legislative Assembly (1849-51).—93.

Véron, Louis Désiré (1798-1867) —French journalist and politician, up to 1848 Orleanist, then Bonapartist; the proprietor of the newspaper Constitutionnel.—134.

Vidal, François (1814-1872)— French economist, petty-bourgeois Socialist, in 1848 Secretary of the Luxemburg Commission, deputy to the Legislative Assembly (1850-51).— 69.

Vieyra—French colonel, in 1851 chief of the general staff of the national Guard; Bonapartist, participated in the coup d'état of December 2, 1851.— 56.